rationalization

possible fraud opportunity

BN DePaul UNV 1E JACKSON,CHICAGO 60604

3525 CASH-1   1175 0001 006

978057802125 NEW
PAPERNY/LESSONS FR   MDS 1   16.00
            SUBTOTAL   16.00
  SALES TAX 10.25%   1.64
              TOTAL   17.64

ACCOUNT NUMBER   XXXXXXXXXXXXX7181
    Visa/Mastercard   17.64
  Expiration Date   XX/XX
    Authorization   040718

    (312)362-8792 depaul.bkstore.com

                        1/26/10 5:12 PM

- A full refund will be given in your original form of payment if general reading books are returned within 14 days of purchase with a receipt.
- After 14 days, no refunds or exchanges.
- No refunds or exchanges without a receipt.
- Books must be in original condition.

ALL OTHER MERCHANDISE:

- A full refund will be given in your original form of payment with a receipt.
- With a receipt, unopened software, CDs, cassettes, VHS tapes, and DVDs may be exchanged or refunded. (Opened software, CDs, cassettes, VHS tapes, and DVDs may be exchanged for the identical item only.)
- Without a receipt, a merchandise credit will be issued at the current selling price.
- Cash back on merchandise credits or gift cards will not exceed $5.
- No refunds on gift cards, prepaid cards, phone cards, or magazines.
- All merchandise must be in original condition.

www.whywaitforbooks.com

Buy Used Save 25%

SAVE THIS RECEIPT

your school.
your bookstore.

REFUND POLICY

TEXTBOOKS:

- A Full Refund will be given in your original form of payment if textbooks are returned during the first week of class with a receipt.
- With a proof of schedule change and a receipt, a full refund will be given in your original form of payment during the first 30 days of classes.

Lessons From Prison

Bear Stearns, UBS Stockbroker Muses
on Ethics and Provides Guide Through
Criminal Justice System

[signature]
Jun 2010

Justin M. Paperny

APS Publishing
California

Lessons From Prison

Bear Stearns, UBS Stockbroker Muses
on Ethics and Provides Guide Through
Criminal Justice System

Justin M. Paperny

APS Publishing
California

With respect and humility, I dedicate
this book to my loving parents,

Tallie and Bernard Paperny

The greatest discovery of my generation is that a human being can alter his life by altering his attitude.

— William James

Justin M. Paperny

Lessons From Prison

BEAR STEARNS, UBS STOCKBROKER MUSES ON ETHICS AND PROVIDES GUIDE THROUGH CRIMINAL JUSTICE SYSTEM

Justin M. Paperny graduated from the University of Southern California in 1997. He built his career as a stockbroker at the firms of Merrill Lynch; Crowell, Weedon and Co.; Bear Stearns; and UBS. Justin's area of expertise focused on managing financial assets for hedge funds and professional athletes.

Despite a privileged background, seven-figure earnings before his 30th birthday, and a promising career in financial services, Justin lost his way. Allowing greed and self-interest to interfere with ethical judgments, Justin stumbled into a Ponzi scheme. Rather than making the values-based decisions for which his background seasoned him, Justin facilitated the fraud.

Through Justin's writings, his speaking, and his podcasts, Justin describes the lessons he learned and the strategies that empowered him to overcome the adversities his own decisions created. For more information, please visit:

JUSTINPAPERNY.COM
JPAPERNY@MAC.COM

Acknowledgements

With a great deal of gratitude, it is a privilege to acknowledge my loving mother, Tallie Paperny. With the considerable investment my mother made in typing my daily blogs, as well as typing the manuscript for this book, my mother served this prison term alongside me. She and her husband, Ken Mayer, spent many hours in Taft's visiting room. I'm stronger because of their steadfast support.

Likewise, I thank my dear father, Bernard Paperny and my stepmother, Ronda Paperny. The ancillary consequences of my imprisonment caused my family a degree of humiliation. Through responses to the problems my actions created, I hope to have taken the initial steps toward atonement. In time, I intend to prove myself worthy of my family's love and support.

I thank my brother Todd and his remarkable wife Sunny. They, too, have endured the struggles and anxieties associated with my confinement. During the time I served, they brought my niece Clover into the world. I pledge to live as a loving, strong, and honorable role model for her, and for all of my family members.

My childhood friend, Brad Fullmer and his wonderful wife Elana, stood beside me as if I were family. Likewise, my friend Sam Pompeo took me into his home when I needed support, and he looked after my interests while I served my sentence. A man could not ask for better friends than Brad, Elana, and Sam.

Many other close friends enabled me not only to persevere, but to thrive through turmoil. They include, but are not limited to Randi Aronson, Chad Calabria, Skip Cooper, Roger Ewing, Melinda Feldman, Nathan Freeman, Cindy Fullerton, Marv and Judy Fullmer, Chris Garza,

Dana Haber, Michael Hayes, Damon and Nikki Johnson, Stacy Kleiner, The Kotkin Family, Andy Levinson, Dr. Alan and Jane Lewis, Julio and Liz Marcial, Nicole Monlon, Todd Morgan, Thomas Morgan, Lorraine Parker, Ken and Anna Pompeo, Lucas Pompeo, Laura Reno, Larry Schneiderman, P.C. Shaw, Michele Stanisch, Ande Stewart, the Stromsborg Family, Bella Susman, Mara and Louie Tapia, the Tipp Family, and Ernie Wish.

Finally, I want to thank Walt Pavlo, who helped me prepare for the journey. And I thank Michael Santos, who collaborated and assisted me in communicating on paper the way I communicate in person.

Despite the help of all the people named above, and those unnamed, I accept full responsibility for all that I express. I remain a work of redemption in progress, and I ask for your patience.

Justin M. Paperny
May 20, 2009

Lessons From Prison

Contents

1
The Beginning

Twelve months in prison helped recalibrate my life. I certainly didn't expect that I would grow from the experience. Yet those anxieties that plagued me during the three years that preceded my confinement were by far the worst part of my journey through the criminal justice system. Like many of the other white-collar offenders I met at Taft's Federal Prison Camp, I simply didn't know all the ways that prison could empower and change my life for the better.

From the beginning, I missed my family, my community, and my dog, Honey. Understandably, those feelings would stay with me through the term. In time, however, I developed routines that helped me feel productive and brought meaning to my life. Instead of struggling with the bad decisions I made that led to my troubles with the law, I spent many hours reflecting, deep in introspection. By figuring out where I had fallen off track, I could take corrective actions.

Clearly, my background suggested much brighter prospects than a stint in federal prison.

My name is Justin Paperny. When I self-surrendered to Taft Prison Camp on 28 April 2008, I was 33-years-old. My parents, Tallie and Bernie, had reared my brother Todd and me in the affluent community of Encino, in the heart of Los Angeles' San Fernando Valley.

Like most American boys, as a youngster I fell in love with baseball. I had a natural gift for the sport, as if I were born with a fielder's glove on my hand. I developed a powerful build as a youngster, and my strength led to many homeruns. I played on all-star teams from the time I turned seven, and during the course of my athletic career, I was fortunate to play in three separate World Series tournaments.

Through baseball, I learned virtues that should have stayed with me throughout life. Good sportsmanship meant loyalty, discipline, integrity, and a sense of balance. It was my childhood coach, Jack Gilardi, who really taught me the importance of such concepts. As a child and young man, those qualities or character traits were integral to my life. They led to my earning distinctions that brought a sense of pride to my parents. Through my success on the baseball diamond, I was invited to attend the prestigious Montclair Preparatory School in Van Nuys. By the time I graduated, I held several records in the Babe Ruth World Series. Those accomplishments led to scholarship offers from some of America's best universities. I chose the University of Southern California.

While playing baseball for USC, I realized that I was no longer in the top tier among athletes. I had been a standout from the time I was six-years-old, though I reached my peak performance as a high school player. The teammates around me were continuing to develop, whereas I had kind of stagnated. At USC, under the outstanding coaching of Mike Gillespie, I worked as hard as I possibly could. Yet I was forced to accept that my unexceptional performance on a team that included many world-class athletes would limit me to a supporting rather than a starring role.

Many players whom I had known since childhood would advance to sterling careers in the major leagues. My closest friend, Brad Fullmer, was drafted by the Montreal Expos after graduation from Montclair Prep. He was one of the very few athletes who homered during his first at bat in the big leagues. Later, Brad was a major contributor to the Anaheim Angels during their 2002 World Series victory.

Other friends of mine, who built huge careers in the big leagues, include Jeff Suppan, Aaron Boone and Geoff Jenkins. I knew that my baseball career would end at USC.

I was in my early 20s, and I understood that without sports I would have to find another way to earn a living. My father owned a hardware store that had been in the family for three generations. My brother Todd, however, who was studying at UCLA, expressed more interest in carrying on the family business. I had to find something else.

Through a friend of my mother's, I became intrigued with the brokerage business. I was majoring in psychology at USC. When I told my mother that I was thinking about becoming a stockbroker, she stepped up to help. That was Tallie's way. She was a wonderful mother, and never missed an opportunity to make my brother and me feel as if our success and happiness were the highest values of her life.

"I have to call your cousin, Richard Levy," she said. "He's highly educated and newspapers have reported him as being one of the most successful brokers on Wall Street."

I'd never met this cousin, yet my mother felt certain he would usher me into the elite world of high finance. Richard, on the other hand, who was a star at Bear Stearns, was underwhelmed with the plea for intervention from my mother. He was based in New York, and he didn't have the time to tutor a distant cousin who wasn't even studying in the Ivy Leagues.

"Why don't you call Todd Goodman," Richard suggested. "Todd's right there in Los Angeles. He should have no problem helping your son get started."

Todd Goodman was another cousin of mine, and he was a money-management legend in his own right. Todd would become the founder of Goodman Investments but at the time my mom called him he was a lead performer in the Los Angeles office of Goldman Sachs. She pleaded with Todd to give me a break. "Have him here by four tomorrow morning. And tell him to wear a suit and tie."

I was on summer break between my junior and senior year when my mom orchestrated my interview with Todd. Although we had never met previously, I knew of his and his brother Jeff's success. Both were partners at Goldman Sachs, and they managed portfolios for some of the biggest names in the entertainment business. When I presented myself to the Goldman Sachs offices at four in the morning, I didn't know what to expect. I found a room bristling with energy and alive with action. Todd stood at the heart of it all.

"So, you're the baseball player," Todd said as he sized me up. "Where do you plan on going to business school?"

"I'm not planning on getting an MBA," I answered. "I want to learn about the brokerage business."

Todd wasn't impressed. "What do you mean, you're not going to business school? You've got to get an MBA."

"I want to be a stockbroker, not an investment banker."

Todd looked at me as if I were a child complaining about school. "A stockbroker's nothing more than a salesman. Maybe you should just sell cars."

"Can't I just learn about stocks from you for a while?"

"What do you want to do?"

"I want to watch you work, to learn about the business a little."

"Okay," Todd told me. "You can watch."

I wouldn't exactly call my time at Goldman Sachs an internship. Still, my time with Todd certainly convinced me that I wanted to build a career as a stockbroker. I loved the excitement. I sat in the trading room listening to the lingo and feeling myself infected with the adrenaline rush. I watched men screaming orders that had values in the tens of millions into the telephone. Although I didn't do much more than pour coffee and lick envelopes, I felt the same level of excitement in that room as if I were playing on a team in a stadium with 20,000 screaming baseball fans and national television was broadcasting the game.

On the advice of Todd, I interned at a few other brokerage houses while I was finishing up my final year at USC. Those efforts paid off. By networking in the industry, I had a few job offers waiting for me once I had my degree in hand. Although Todd's influence helped me secure an interview with Goldman in New York, I understood that was not enough. Moderately good grades and a baseball pedigree from a California school were not going to get me beyond the first round of interviews at the world's most prestigious investment bank. As my interviewer told me in no uncertain terms, "Goldman typically hires only from the Ivies, and we only accept students of exceptional distinction."

Within a week of graduating, I accepted a job offer to work at Merrill Lynch in Orange County. In order to ensure that I could make it to the office before five each morning, I moved 60 miles south. By the second day I felt miserable. I missed my girlfriend, my family, and my home.

The job required that I stay in the office from well before dawn until after nine each evening. The job wasn't even fulfilling. I hadn't yet earned my securities license so I was restricted to cold calling and sending out research materials. Other brokers referred to my tasks as paying dues. Being a team player, I felt willing and eager to give

19

the job all I had. Within weeks, however, the pressures were wreaking havoc on my personal life.

I had graduated college in tip-top physical condition, lean and muscular. That changed quickly after I started my career as a stockbroker. The long hours left zero time for exercise. During the day, I would chow down the catered meals brought into the brokerage house. When I finished in the evening, I gorged myself with more pizza, burgers, or burritos from fast food restaurants. Within months, my weight had ballooned by 30 pounds, none of it muscle.

"You could lose 15 pounds just in your cheeks," my girlfriend would tease during my weekend trips home.

"What the hell are you doing down there?" My friend, Brad, would look at me with astonishment. Health magazines had given him cover shots as baseball's most fit athlete. "You've only been out of college for a few months, and you already look like an old man. I don't know what's going on down in O.C., but you need to mix in a salad once in a while. It's time to boycott In-and-Out."

They were right. I was working myself to death and I felt miserable. I studied for my Series Seven exam with the appropriate agency for securities professionals, and I earned my license a few months later.

Once I had my license in hand, I learned the truth about the brokerage business. It was cut throat. Unlike my experience as a baseball player, where men of good character and fairness surrounded me, in the brokerage business I was living amidst deceit, greed, and questionable ethics.

I was only 23-years-old when my supposed sponsoring partners at Merrill Lynch shafted me for commissions to which I was rightfully entitled. From that treachery, I learned that I would have to play by a new set of rules to make it as a broker.

I left Merrill Lynch in anger because I felt cheated out of several thousand dollars of commissions. If neither the firm nor my colleagues would stand by me, I saw no reason to stand by loyally to them.

In retrospect, I recognize that my decision to leave Merrill was one of the first in a series of sliders. I felt my moral character deteriorating. Rather than standing up for fairness, integrity, and discipline, and the other virtues I had been groomed to follow as an athlete, I began my descent to the lowest common denominator in the brokerage business.

Instead of promoting and living by a solid code of ethics, I compromised my own values and ceased to function as a team player. I allowed myself to become influenced by the worst part of the industry, meaning that I thought about my own short-term needs rather than the greater good of the team and a winning season.

It was similar to my decision not to earn an MBA, as my cousin Todd Goodman had urged me to pursue. All of those years committing myself to baseball, I suppose, had taken a toll on my ability to focus on delayed gratification. I felt less inclined to look into the future and commit to further investment of time. I had reached my early 20s and felt ready to get paid.

Ironically, it wasn't until I came to prison that I began to see those traits. The more than 12 months I spent locked inside the community of felons gave me the space I needed for introspection. By realizing where and how I had gone wrong, I could understand my weaknesses better. That self-awareness made a difference in my adjustment. It gave me better direction for the rest of my life.

2
The Fraud Triangle

I had been at Merrill Lynch for one year when I quit in a huff. At the time, I had built a book of business, which was just south of $10 million dollars under management, most of which came from family, friends, and acquaintances. The sum wasn't a large amount in the brokerage world, yet it was sufficient to ensure that I could walk into any moderate sized brokerage house and negotiate an employment offer.

I chose Crowell, Weedon and Co., the largest regional firm on the West Coast. Richard Jacobson was the manager of the Encino branch, and he welcomed me with open arms. Many of the other brokers were set in their ways, stodgy, too tired to chase new accounts. Jacobson saw hunger in my eyes and hired me on the spot. I was 24-years-old and he offered me a guaranteed salary that was three times as much as what I was earning at Merrill, plus a commission split that assured I would earn six figures in my first year. I was chasing the money.

While at Crowell, Weedon I worked the phone and I worked the streets. By cold calling and cold walking I picked up every account I could find, adding tens of thousands to my assets under management each week. I had my spiel down, promising to deliver the world while not giving a thought to asset allocation or the client's specific needs. My approach differed in remarkable ways from Todd Goodman, who cultivated long-term relationships by recommending slow and steady growth.

Within months, I became one of the top producing brokers in the branch office. I learned some sharp-elbowed practices from Keith Gilabert, a fellow broker. He taught me how to earn higher commissions by churning accounts, how to finagle free lunches out of mutual funds, and he introduced me to a few other tricks that would boost my monthly production to the long-term detriment of my career.

The branch manager loved my performance and encouraged the aggressive tactics. I felt experienced, ready to advance on to the bigger players by tapping into my network of professional athletes. I contacted my friend, Dan Lozano, from the well-known Beverly Hills Sports Council.

Dan was an alumni of USC, and he had cultivated relationships with professional baseball players. Knowing that he represented such players as Mike Piazza, José Canseco, and Barry Bonds, I called him for a lunch date with hopes of persuading him to introduce me to his clients, so that I could sell them on my skills as a money manager.

"Here's the deal," Lozano told me during our lunch. "Kenny Sorosky is my close friend. We were fraternity brothers and roommates at USC. He's a broker at Bear and he gets all my guys."

We continued the discussion, and by the end of the meal, Lozano agreed to set up a meeting between Kenny and me. Kenny was a few years older, a fellow Trojan, and we both had grown up in Encino. Lozano thought an opportunity might exist for Kenny and me to partner. I sensed the upside of linking my business with Kenny's. If he could open the door at a brand-name firm like Bear Stearns, and introduce me to the trade of managing money for professional athletes, I knew my career had more potential to rocket.

Kenny and I hit it off during our meeting. He introduced me to David Pollock, the branch manager of

Bear Stearns in Century City. When David heard that Kenny wanted me to join Bear so that we could work together as partners, he agreed to grant an interview. I only had about $15 million under management, and less than two years experience as a broker. Those were not the types of credentials that opened doors at first-tier investment houses such as Bear Stearns. Nevertheless, during our interview, I let it pop that my cousin was Todd Goodman of Goodman Investments and that Richard Levy was another distant cousin.

Those family relationships erased any reluctance David Pollock may have had about hiring me. Goodman Investments would not accept accounts of less than $25 million and David understood that as Todd's young cousin, there was an excellent chance that Todd would refer accounts to me if they did not meet his minimum criteria. Pollack offered a compensation package, and without giving Jacobson at Crowell, Weedon a chance to counter, I submitted my letter of resignation, taking all of my accounts with me. My loyalty, I felt, was to my career, not to the team of Crowell, Weedon and Co.

With only $15 million under management, I accepted the role of junior partner to Kenny Sorosky, who managed more than $40 million of investor assets. That relationship left me with a smaller portion of the revenue split when we were distributing commissions. Although I agreed to the terms of the partnership, I grew to resent my status as the junior partner.

I felt as if my contributions warranted a higher payout. I was on track to earn north of $200,000 during my first year with Kenny; our partnership agreement, however, entitled Kenny to rake in more than three times as much. The revenue split to which I had agreed was not sitting well.

24

Lessons From Prison

I had brought in an incredibly lucrative hedge fund as an account. That fund was kicking off as much as $100,000 a month in trading commissions. Despite the efforts I made to win the account, and the work I was performing to manage the heavy volume of trades, the partnership agreement gave Kenny the lion's share of the commission split.

My sense of being under appreciated and under compensated failed to move Kenny. As the senior broker, he felt entitled to the higher split. After all, he insisted, his influence was the reason Bear Stearns had hired me.

At 25, I was the youngest broker Bear had ever hired in its Los Angeles office. According to Kenny, that never would have happened without his sponsorship. He told me that I still had dues to pay, that both patience and gratitude would suit me well.

Although I agreed to continue with our arrangement, beneath the surface I could feel Kenny exploiting me. When I spotted an opportunity to even the playing field, I took it. Those actions, I now recognize, represented my succumbing to what others have called the fraud triangle. It's a trap that can lead to moral failure, a slippery slope that frequently lands people in prison.

With the fraud triangle, the individual feels the pressure. He feels as if he is being cheated, or as if he needs to overcome some hurdle. The hurdle may present itself in the form of the need for a higher income to pay an obligation, or even some desire to advance one's standing.

In my case, I resented the concept that I had to pay dues. I was bringing in the money. I felt entitled to respect and to more compensation. Without that perceived sense of fairness, I felt as if my colleague was taking advantage of me. In my mind, that injustice could not stand.

25

The second prong of the fraud triangle was the rationalization. In my case, since I felt as if I were being cheated, it only seemed fair that I take what was rightfully mine.

As an athlete, if I ever felt the manager wasn't recognizing my performance, I could work harder. My stats would easily convince him that I deserved a higher position in the batting order. Either way, I recognized the importance of the team first, and accepted that our team's manager had a reason for his decision.

As a cynical money manager on the other hand, that sense of fair play I had learned through sports didn't mean as much. The partnership agreement I had made with Kenny failed to reflect my performance. With his response that I needed to pay my dues, I rationalized that he was looking out for himself rather than for my interest as a contributing team player. Since he wasn't interested in being fair to me, I rationalized that I would look out for myself.

The third prong of the fraud triangle was opportunity. I felt pressure by the perceived lack of fairness.

Even though I was earning an income far beyond the grasp of most young men, I felt my performance entitled me to more. I rationalized the unfairness. The opportunity presented itself to bank some full commissions, in total violation of the partnership agreement I had made with Kenny. In my mind it was all fair. That type of thinking differed in remarkable ways from the values of a sportsman, but it seemed acceptable with my sliding scale of ethics. It was the strangling triangle of pressure, rationalization, and opportunity that eventually led me to fraud.

Lessons From Prison

As a prisoner in a minimum-security federal prison camp, I met and interacted with hundreds of men who served time for white-collar crimes. Some engaged in securities fraud. Others launched businesses that turned into Ponzi schemes. I knew men who manipulated records in transparent and ultimately futile attempts to evade taxes. The crimes may have varied, but the motivation for each, without exception, followed the familiar pattern of pressure, rationalization, and opportunity, the fraud triangle. I came to this conclusion as I began to think of a neighbor in an adjacent cubicle.

Steve and I had walked around the dirt track earlier that evening. He told me that he had been the controller for a moderately sized and privately held company, which distributed industrial parts. He'd been with the company for more than a decade and thought that his contributions enabled the firm to grow its customer base exponentially. The owner relied on Steve to manage the operations, but Steve felt as if the owner neglected to share in the profits. Steve told me that he was entitled to a higher percentage of the annual bonus pool, yet the owner of the firm declined to offer an equitable distribution.

Steve controlled both the billing and receivables. He also prepared the monthly income statement and balance sheet. Those responsibilities offered Steve ample opportunity to cheat his employer.

He launched his fraud by opening a straw business with a name that was eerily familiar to his employer's. Steve also opened a bank account with the straw company's name. Each month, he would deposit checks that rightfully belonged to his employer into this straw account. Over time, those thefts amounted to hundreds of thousands of dollars. As the financial controller of a private company with millions in monthly revenues, Steve had the opportunity to execute his fraud easily.

Auditors eventually detected his crime and he served a four-year sentence. The irony was that as Steve told me the story, he remained adamant that he didn't take anything to which he wasn't entitled. Despite the prison term, Steve was still stuck in the fraud triangle. In my opinion, that refusal to accept responsibility kept Steve locked in a negative adjustment pattern. We as individuals had to learn and grow from our decisions.

By diverting commissions from Kenny's and my joint account and routing them to my personal account, I was able to even the short-term score. With an extra ten thousand here, an extra fifteen thousand there, I could take care of myself even if the partnership wouldn't. Those types of decisions violated a code of ethics that led to long-term success. Worse, they made it easier to succumb further into the fraud triangle.

3
Our Ponzi at Bear Stearns and UBS

After a year at Bear Stearns, Kenny and I jumped ship. By then, using the prestige of the Bear Stearns name, we were able to build a book of business that specialized in discretionary accounts for professional athletes, and offered trading services to small hedge funds. We had more than $100 million under management. That sum was sufficient to persuade the rival firm of UBS to offer our partnership a seven-figure signing bonus if we would ditch Bear Stearns to bring our clients to UBS.

I followed my partner out of Bear Stearns in pursuit of a signing bonus that would put an immediate six figure sum in my pocket. Despite my payday, I didn't feel a sense of pride or honor in my actions. Rather, I felt sleazy inside, as if I were the embodiment of selling out. Had I called my cousin, Todd Goodman at Goodman Investments, he would have been disappointed. A decision to sacrifice a potentially distinguished career for a signing bonus, in his eyes, was along the same lines as my decision to forego graduate school and jump-start my career as a stockbroker.

Knowing that Todd would disapprove of my decision, I did not pay him the courtesy of a phone call. I simply lacked the courage because deep inside I did not feel worthy of the mentoring he had tried to give me. As I rode the elevator down the Century City Towers from Bear Stearns' trading center on the 30th floor, I hoped that I wouldn't run into Todd, whose office was in the same building.

At UBS, my career with Kenny followed the same pattern. We pursued short term trading profits through high commission trades. One of Kenny's master scams to swindle hundreds of thousands in extra commissions was churning trades without our client's consent. As a team at large brokerage houses like Bear Stearns and UBS, we were constantly flipping our clients through syndicate deals. The clients were supposed to authorize such trades, but Kenny knew which clients wouldn't notice; we would dump on them to build higher commissions. This strategy was both unethical and illegal, though it was a common practice in my experience with Kenny. We were more like bookies than professional money managers, more interested with banking profits for UBS and ourselves than for our clients.

At UBS our client list focused primarily on professional athletes and hedge funds. In time, our assets under management grew to exceed $200 million. I had connived my way into earnings of more than $1 million before I reached my 28th birthday.

Rather than take pride in my career, I felt a sense of self-loathing. Within a few months of leaving college, poor eating habits and the lack of exercise transformed my athletic build into a blob of putty. I smoked incessantly. Instead of striving to boost the value of my partnership with Kenny, I stewed with resentment and feelings that our agreed commission split failed to reflect my true worth.

I didn't give a thought to any allegiance I may have owed to Bear Stearns for the investment the firm made in my career. On the first day as a Bear Stearns account executive, the legendary Ace Greenberg called to welcome and wish me success. With the distinction my distant cousins earned on Wall Street in general, and at Bear Stearns in particular, the firm's leadership had high hopes for the development of my career.

While in prison, my reflections convinced me that I had let the team of Bear Stearns down in a big way. I was 26-years-old and deeply under the influence of my senior partner, Kenny Sorosky. He had made some speculative investments that turned out badly. After having lost a significant amount of his capital, Kenny began shopping the street for a better deal. Specifically, he wanted the infusion of capital that came with a signing bonus. Kenny found that deal in an adjacent building, in the office of UBS.

Without a moment's forewarning, Kenny shocked David Pollock, our branch manager at Bear Stearns. Kenny told David that he was quitting the team for a better offer at UBS. Pollock was livid and felt betrayed. I made matters worse by handing Pollock my resignation as well. He looked at me as if I were a traitor, deserving of every contemptuous and profane word in his outburst.

I walked out of Bear Stearns feeling foolish and embarrassed. At that time I had been a broker for four years. The decisions I had made were inconsistent with the character and discipline I had learned as an athlete. I left Merrill Lynch because of a dispute over commissions. At Crowell, Weedon, Richard Jacobson had been grooming me for leadership. After a year, however, I sneaked away without even having had the courage to confront him face-to-face. Instead, I simply resigned with a note and began my career at Bear Stearns. Even in that pursuit, I traded more on the names of my distinguished cousins than on my own merits.

Two of the most significant casualties in my pursuit of short-term earnings were the cultivation of trust and loyalty. Those virtues represent the core of any winning team. They did not have a place in my partnership with Kenny or in my career. We were not loyal to the firms we represented, to our clients, to each other or to ourselves. The low level of trust between us led to a lack of fulfillment in my career, and to an accelerating downward spiral of my self-perception as an individual.

Keith Gilabert ran the GLT Venture Fund, one of the small hedge funds I had cultivated as a client. I had known Keith before he launched his hedge fund. We had shared space at Crowell, Weedon where he had begun his career as a broker. I had known him to hold a loose code of ethics then, but those perceptions did not dissuade me from accepting the GLT Venture Fund as an account and source of trading commissions.

My eventual criminal conviction may have had its roots in the demise of my values that began after college. It was my relationship with Gilabert that actually pushed me over the line.

The GLT Fund had been a relatively small account with only $5 million under management. Keith was perhaps the worst stock picker in the history of money management. His fund lost value for investors with every undisciplined trade. Through false representations to prospective clients, Keith continued to bring new money into the account. He generated substantial commissions for Kenny and me, sometimes surpassing six figures in a single month.

Keith's losses with the GLT Fund were so magnificent that they spawned a new trading strategy for my partner, Kenny Sorosky.

"If Keith goes long a stock," Kenny suggested, "We're going to sell it short. If he shorts a stock, let's take it long immediately."

We didn't need to know anything more about an investment other than the position Keith had taken. The irony was that by betting against our client, we profited handsomely.

Our superiors at UBS understood the unsustainability of Gilabert's GLT Fund. Nevertheless, the global management firm was itself caught up with the pursuit of short-term profits. Rather than protecting the incredible investment of trust and good will in the UBS brand, our superiors at UBS cautioned Kenny and me to protect us from litigation.

We all knew that the individual investors in Gilabert's hedge fund were losing significant amounts of money. The commissions generated by the fund, however, were too great to ignore. Despite the consistent flow of losses, new investors poured millions into the fund's account. To protect us and UBS, Kenny and I generated a disclosure letter that notified GLT Fund investors that Keith Gilabert, and not any UBS money managers, was responsible for the fund's performance.

My experiences as a professional money manager left me with the impression that all relationships were based on deceit, rather than trust. The single exception was my cousin, Todd Goodman.

Rather than striving to hoodwink clients in pursuit of short-term profit, Todd created lifetime partnerships. He cultivated relationships, imbuing a sense of trust with those around him. Todd's steady hand helped people feel confident that he would protect their assets for future generations. Kenny and I, on the other hand, were making irresponsible decisions that would lead us to higher monthly performance targets.

Keith Gilabert's GLT Fund had reduced itself to a Ponzi scheme. The intention to defraud may not have existed at the outset, as Keith likely set out to achieve high returns for investors in his fund. He speculated, however, combining investor money with borrowed funds using a three-to-one leverage. In other words, margin loans we made available at UBS allowed Keith to take $15 million dollar positions on stocks when he only had $5 million of investor money. With his track record of taking losing positions, investor money evaporated faster than an early-morning mist.

Our experience in the brokerage business gave Kenny and me, as well as our superiors at UBS, sufficient reason to believe that Keith was misrepresenting the dismal performance of his GLT Fund. Despite massive losses, he continued to attract new investor money. At UBS, we neglected our instincts and instead took the position of the figurative monkeys who saw no evil, spoke no evil, and heard no evil.

Kenny once asked one of Gilabert's investors why the investor was depositing $4 million into the GLT hedge fund. The investor looked Kenny in the eye and said, "You've seen the rate of return the fund is delivering. Performance sells itself." That investor's rationale should have led to additional inquiries from Kenny and me about what "performance" meant to the investor.

By that time Kenny and I both knew that Gilabert had lost millions. Nevertheless, we accepted the $4 million deposit and agreed between ourselves that we would never ask an investor for his rational again. "That way," Kenny said, "we will never have to acknowledge that we knew anything."

Our efforts to maintain plausible deniability, however, crumbled during a meeting I agreed to take with Keith and Abe, one of the major investors of the GLT Fund. Abe was a rabbi who was 90-years-old. A team of Abe's accountants and financial advisors wanted to meet with the principals behind the GLT Fund. Their efforts at due diligence were to ease their concerns about Abe's asset allocation. Gilabert asked me to attend the meeting in order to represent the gravitas of UBS. Knowing what I knew then about the fund, I should not have walked into that meeting.

"Does UBS think it wise that a 90-year-old rabbi would invest his life's savings, $3 million, into a basket of growth stocks?" The accountant directed his question to me.

At that moment, I felt like the proverbial deer that had been unexpectedly caught in the headlights. I scratched my head. I knew that as of the morning of our meeting, the GLT Fund had a total asset balance of less than $1 million. If Abe's financial advisory team believed that Abe had $3 million invested in the GLT Fund, then clearly, Keith Gilabert had provided them with fraudulent account statements. Rather than expose the troubling discrepancy, I ducked the question.

"No," I answered. "UBS is the custodian of the GLT account. As our letter of disclosure indicated, Keith Gilabert is solely responsible for allocating client assets."

"We understand that," the accountant persisted, "but would UBS recommend that an elderly client invest his life savings in growth stocks?"

"Although we don't presume to know the investment strategies of those in the GLT Fund, at UBS we typically would recommend a much more conservative allocation for an elderly gentleman. We would include a much higher percentage of government bonds that offered a fixed-income stream."

In continuously trying to dodge the advisors' questions, I was lying. Their inquiries gave tangible proof that Gilabert was perpetuating a fraud. I appeased Abe and his investment advisers with assurances that I would assist Gilabert in restructuring the account. Yet when Gilabert

35

Justin M. Paperny

and I were finally alone, I realized the magnitude of my deception. I had become complicitous in his scheme.

"What did you do to me?" I was livid with Gilabert.

"Please," he pleaded. "Just help me get through this. I have some new accounts coming in that will set things right with Abe. I can make it up."

Gilabert was using new investor money to cover losses. He had built a house of cards, and the scheme was about to come crashing down. I didn't know how I could escape unscathed.

Over the course of the next several months, Kenny and I allowed Gilabert to deepen the Ponzi scheme. The more investor money he brought in, the more trading commissions we stood to reap. With investor losses continuing to mount, however, it was only a matter of time before someone would expose the financial crimes of which I had become an integral part. Although I rationalized my complicity with excuses that I was only giving Gilabert an opportunity to break even with investors, in reality, I wanted the gravy train of easy and exorbitant commissions to continue.

I had hoped to last through June of 2006, when more than a quarter million dollars worth of bonus incentives UBS allotted to me would have vested. That was my target date. If I could skate through to receive that windfall, I reasoned, I could grab the money and leave the brokerage business.

My good friend, Sam Pompeo, was a successful real estate agent who offered me an opportunity to partner with him. I wanted to make that career switch, to leave the dirt I had created in the brokerage business behind and begin anew.

The break I was looking for, however, did not come so easily. In December of 2004, investors from the GLT

36

Fund called my superiors at UBS to confirm account balances. Those calls led to my termination as a UBS employee. At the time, my biggest regret was that I had not been able to hang on. I didn't consider the troubling reality that my actions had violated securities laws.

4
Self-Delusions, Lies, and Attorneys

In my capacity as a broker for UBS, I knew that Gilabert lost investors' money with nearly each individual trade. Motivated by the exorbitant high commissions the account generated, I had a myopic interest in keeping the fund alive. The lax oversight violated the rules of ethics and the principles of good business. The greed, however, was not yet a violation of the law.

When I sat in on that meeting with Keith Gilabert, his client Abe, and Abe's advisors, I had indisputable evidence that Gilabert had been conning Abe. My presence at the meeting bolstered Gilabert's credibility, which contributed to the fraud. Then, I clearly perpetuated the fraud when I allowed Abe and his advisors to believe that Abe's asset balance had a $3 million valuation. At that point, I became more than an unscrupulous broker. My failure to act and set the record straight violated the law.

Upon losing my employment at UBS, I wasn't prepared to own up to the full magnitude of my problems. Kenny, my partner, was more savvy, or Machiavellian about such matters. He retained counsel and began negotiations to protect his position with UBS and immune himself from all liabilities associated with the GLT Fund.

Likewise, Keith Gilabert had lawyered up. He had cut a cooperation agreement with prosecutors to minimize his exposure to prison time. I had not yet reached my 30th year, and was not wise or cynical enough in the ways of the world to appreciate the depth of my troubles.

Rather than consult with a criminal attorney, I hired a civil attorney upon my termination from UBS. Losing my job had exposed me to potential financial penalties in relation to prepaid bonus money I had received. I wanted counsel to advise me through those employment issues. When the lawyers began a thread of inquiries into the reasons behind my termination, however, I dissembled. I feigned ignorance of the fraud to which I knew had occurred, and to which I had come to play a peripheral role.

My lack of honesty with the civil attorney was the first in a long series of bad decisions I made following my termination from UBS. I paid a steep price for my refusal to come clean and accept responsibility. Being ignorant of the consequences, I tried to cover up my culpability with lies. One lie led to another.

I took that ridiculous approach in a futile attempt to spare myself the embarrassing and humiliating consequences of my actions. I didn't want my mother to know that her son had been complicitous in a fraud nor did I want my reputation to suffer. Clinging to my denial only exacerbated my struggles. Inside, I felt myself a cipher.

In lying to the civil attorney I hired to counsel me, I deprived him of the ability to advise me properly. I had paid him a $5,000 retainer initially to represent me on potential civil litigation related to my employment. As the complexity of the case blossomed, with the reviewing of emails that numbered in the hundreds, with the discussions behind every transaction of the GLT Fund, with the consultations over the purposes behind the disclosure letters we generated to protect UBS from liability, my legal expenses grew to surpass $50,000 with the civil attorney. With all the lies I had told him, however, the guidance he provided was not what my predicament warranted.

As the months dragged on, my civil problems that I had mistakenly believed related to my employment, escalated to inquiries from the SEC and FBI. Because of the lies I had told my attorney, he assured me that I didn't have to worry about the federal investigators of the GLT Fund. "Just be honest," my attorney advised. "Tell them everything you've told me and you will be fine."

When I met with the Department of Justice attorneys, I told the same lies that had been sustaining me from the beginning. I had lied so often that I almost believed the lies myself. I couldn't have been at fault, I reasoned. Gilabert was the criminal, not me. I simply executed the trades at his direction. In telling both half-truths and some outright lies to the government attorneys, I was committing new criminal conduct. Prosecutors, I later learned, could charge me with lying to officers of the court, and obstructing justice. Those criminal charges could have been in addition to the sanctions I faced for violating securities laws.

In time, prosecutors notified me through my civil attorney that they intended to indict me on a number of criminal charges. With that news, he told me that I would have to retain new counsel. The $50,000 that I had paid to keep the lies alive with my civil attorney had been a total waste. In paying for criminal attorneys to represent me, I burned through more than $200,000.

On a personal level, as I lay on my prison rack, with only concrete and steel around me, I came to realize how my irresponsible actions ripped my core asunder. In time I became unrecognizable from the type of person my parents had tried to groom. Rather than a man of character, temperance and integrity, I was undisciplined. I was a liar and I was a cheat. When events beyond my control threatened to expose me, I made decisions that sunk me deeper. As a consequence, I paid a heavier price for my wrongs. Worse than that, the decisions I made brought both pain and shame to those who loved me.

During those 12-plus months of reflection, I realized that my struggles began long before I ever met Keith Gilabert. I had been honest and disciplined as a child. My commitment to baseball instilled those traits in me. They brought a sense of confidence and self-pride. After ending my baseball career and graduating from USC, however, I moved away from my comfort zone. That was when my ethical slide began. Eventually, that ends-justified-the-means attitude led to my criminal conviction.

Within months, I had fallen off course. Away from home to launch my career in the high-stakes game of money management, I felt levels of stress that challenged my sense of security. I began unhealthy eating habits that led to weight gain. I smoked a pack of cigarettes each day. I didn't exercise at all. My values deteriorated as I was exposed to the worst elements of the brokerage business.

By the time my superiors at UBS fired me, my moral compass was so far askew that I could not bring myself to terms with my predicament. Instead, I created a series of elaborate lies to explain the changes in my life.

When I met with my parents, I lied and said that I had chosen to resign from UBS to pursue a career in real estate. The abrupt change startled them for obvious reasons. They knew that I had obligations and responsibilities. I was 30-years-old. Investments had boosted my net worth to roughly a million dollars. My monthly living expenses exceeded $6,000, and my parents knew that making a change in my career at that stage seemed awfully shaky.

"Why would you take a job in real estate?" My mother was skeptical. "You're a stockbroker."

"I just felt that this was time for me to make a change," I lied. "The whole hedge fund industry was under pressure, and I really grew tired of chasing accounts. I was the junior partner with Kenny, and with the downturn in the market, someone was going to take some blame. Since I wanted to move in a different direction, I just decided to leave UBS."

"But what about the advance bonus you were paid?" My father expressed concern about my financial stability. "Will you have to return the money?"

"Oh no," I lied. I didn't have any clarification regarding that complication. "I parted ways amicably and I'll keep the bonus. This has been a good thing."

My mother looked at me as if she knew I was lying, but she didn't press. Perhaps she instinctively understood that I was under severe stress, and in her love she didn't want to break me. I felt as if I were a four-year-old who had been caught stealing. Not wanting to acknowledge that her angel of a son had committed an act of theft, however, my mom stood silent to accept my story.

Besides my family, I lied to friends. Brad Fullmer had been my closest friend since childhood. Presumably, there was not a single subject I could not discuss openly and honestly with him. Even with Brad, though, I lived in total denial. I just couldn't bring myself to admit to anyone that I had been fired.

Inside, however, I was falling apart. I quit shaving, ate like a glutton and smoked like a fiend. I would lie in my bed at night, traumatized by the rapidly escalating severity of my problems. It seemed as if every week brought more evidence that I was going down. Like an ostrich, however, I ignored all the signs and continued to perpetuate the lie.

At nearly midnight several times each week, I would throw back the covers from my bed. Unable to sleep, I pulled on some sweats and slippers, and then drove to the local In-and-Out Burger. I'd order two double cheeseburgers, a chocolate milkshake, and two orders of large fries. Then I would return home and chow down while I played online chess matches until the early hours of the morning.

To boost my spirits during the day, I deluded myself by playing golf as if I didn't have a care in the world. Ryan, one of my close friends, was from a distinguished Southern California family. We had played baseball together since we were six-years-old and played through USC together. I asked Ryan and his family to sponsor me for membership in the prestigious Lakeside Country Club. I was clinging to the hope that I could erase my troubles by creating a façade of respectability.

As a federal prisoner, I came to understand that living in denial was a common response for white-collar offenders. It seemed that no man wanted to accept that he had engaged in behavior that legislators deemed criminal. While in prison, I met mortgage brokers, bankers, lawyers and businessmen who initially responded to signs that their world was about to implode with decisions that compounded their troubles. Had I known more about how their dramas unfolded, I would have acted differently.

This utter incapability to accept responsibility was like lying on a table with the sword of Damocles swinging back and forth above my neck. I wanted to change the direction of my life, but I couldn't bring myself to acknowledge that I had participated in actions that I knew were fraudulent. People had been hurt as a consequence of my blind pursuit of higher commission earnings. I appeased my conscience by denying that I owed a fiduciary responsibility to the clients Keith had solicited for the GLT Fund. I couldn't bring myself to accept that on account of my misrepresentations, a 90-year-old rabbi had lost more than $3 million.

Even after retaining new counsel, who specialized in white-collar crime, I tried to minimize my exposure to the fraud that I knew had taken place. After lengthy debriefing sessions consumed tens of thousands in legal fees, my lead attorney sent an email to my Blackberry. He insisted that I fly to San Francisco the following week to sit for a lie detector test. He said the strategy was to obtain something tangible we could use as leverage to open negotiations with the government.

"Answer all the questions truthfully," my attorney admonished me. "Don't try to fool the machine. For one thing, it won't work. For another, lies will only bring you more problems."

With the civil attorney I had retained initially, I lied from the start. That approach resulted in burning through $50,000 in legal fees for counsel on irrelevant matters, and my committing new felonies by lying to attorneys who worked for the Department of Justice. The consequences of those lies, however, were not enough to shake me free from the haze of denial. I continued clinging to the illusion that I could somehow manage this disaster. While working with the new criminal attorneys, I again offered half-truths, trying to dance around questions that would portray me negatively.

Upon learning of the upcoming lie-detector test, I immediately Googled for information on polygraph examinations. I found a treasure trove of content, all promising quick-study courses that would teach anyone how to fool the machine. Despite my attorneys' warning on the perils of prevarication, lying, I believed, would help me stay alive. Eagerly, I charged $350 to my credit card to download the course.

For several hours each day, preceding my scheduled exam, I studied through ostensibly proven techniques to beat the test. By tightening my sphincter when answering questions, I supposedly could manipulate the machine's findings of truth to suit my purpose. I had worked through the course so methodically, and practiced so fervently, that when I walked into the San Francisco office where my test had been scheduled, I felt totally confident.

When the questions began, I performed brilliantly. I tensed where I was supposed to tense; I squeezed my innards when appropriate. In the end, the former FBI agent who presided over the exam gave me disappointing results. He said the machine indicated with an accuracy measurement of better than 99.99 percent that I was lying. As I deflated into my chair, my attorney looked at me with concern, and then told the polygraph administrator that he wanted a moment alone with me.

"Justin," he said while sitting across from me, "you're going to prison. It's time to wrap your mind around that reality. You're on incredibly weak ground here. The government prosecutors are prepared to charge you with numerous felonies, including obstruction of justice."

"What does that mean?"

"That means ten years in prison. This is not a game. If you don't come to terms with the seriousness of these problems, we can't help you. You must trust us to look after your interests, and you must give us complete honesty."

At that moment, I suddenly realized how suicide seemed a viable option for so many. I didn't think I could serve a single day in prison. Ten years, for me, was not an option.

Following my return home, I began drowning in depression. An ordeal that could have been resolved much more painlessly with honesty had blown out of proportion. For months, the complications with my case consumed me. My mother sensed my deteriorating spirits and insisted I see a psychiatrist. I began a series of therapy sessions and medication that cost me $1,200 a month. Had I been truthful from the start, I could have responded to my problems much more effectively.

5
Cooperating with the Feds

Finally, more than two years after UBS fired me, I had had enough. I began to correct the bad decisions I had been making. Refusing to continue the charade, I agreed to plead guilty to one count of conspiracy to commit wire fraud, mail fraud, and securities fraud. Those criminal charges exposed me to the possibility of five years in prison.

Had I understood the severity of my problems from the beginning, I could have taken proactive steps to avoid my two-year slide into the abyss. I was naive, oblivious to the treachery and self-preservation I would encounter from my colleagues. While I made the bad decision to dissemble and try to minimize culpability, Keith Gilabert had his own agenda. He was the principal behind the GLT Hedge Fund. Gilabert was also a duplicitous fraud. He wove sinuous stories into what became a preposterous effort to fool prosecutors into believing that my partner and I were part and parcel to every egregious act he committed.

Besides Keith Gilabert's patently absurd efforts to deceive prosecutors, my partner and mentor, Kenny Sorosky surreptitiously schemed behind my back to protect himself while hanging me out as a scapegoat.

Although Kenny was the lead partner and commandeered 50 percent of the commissions generated by Gilabert's GLT Hedge Fund, Sorosky slithered his way into an agreement that allowed him to return to his position with UBS and avoid criminal prosecution, all in exchange for yet one more black blemish on an unscrupulous soul.

Justin M. Paperny

Meanwhile, during the two years that I struggled to regain my sanity, officers at UBS plotted to shield the global investment bank from liability. All of those forces machinated, together and independently, to protect themselves from the harshness of justice while simultaneously forcing my demise.

In the end, prosecutors developed a clearer understanding of all that transpired. They found Gilabert's self-serving explanations implausible when they discovered his ongoing deceptions. As a consequence, they rescinded the cooperation agreement his lawyers had negotiated and charged Gilabert with new criminal conduct. Officials at UBS skated by with an agreement to pay more than $6 million to compensate for loses investors had suffered in the GLT Hedge Fund. Kenny Sorosky kept his bonuses and commissions, but forfeited his conscience.

Prosecutors wanted me to corroborate the evidence they had pieced together from all the snakes in the pit. In contemplating the dilemma of whether to assist government attorneys with the investigation, I sought counsel from my attorney.

"This cooperating," I asked, "does this make me a rat?"

"Why do you ask? Have you been watching *The Sopranos*?"

"Well, you say that by cooperating I may serve time in prison. I've heard that those with the reputation of being rats serve more difficult sentences."

"We can't undo the past, Justin. Had you been the first to accept responsibility, and told the truth from the beginning, you could have been the one with the immunity agreement. You're coming to the party two years late. It's not too late, but it's late. We can't say for certain what kind of sentence you will serve, but if you're truthful, you likely will serve your time in a minimum-security camp with nonviolent offenders."

I had to make a decision, and I chose to cooperate. That was the decision I should have made from the start. After all, I was wrong. I had agreed to facilitate Gilabert's swindle. When I came to learn that he was bringing in new money from unsuspecting investors to cover losses with other investors, I should have reported such illegal manipulations to my superior and to authorities. By the time I had become aware of the fraud, I was in too deep, trapped. Seduced by instant gratification, I seized opportunities as they presented themselves; I rationalized away my culpability.

While serving time in federal prison, I met many men who pleaded guilty to white-collar crimes. We walked around the track together, exercised together, and discussed the decisions we had made. Without exception, each white-collar offender with whom I spoke regretted that he didn't know more about the options available.

I began writing with hopes of filling that void, and as a form of therapy while working through the sentence. As my attorney told me, the best cooperation agreements came to those who accepted full responsibility the soonest. Equally important to receiving the least onerous sanction, however, I found value in the catharsis that came with honesty. During those first two years that followed my abrupt termination as an executive at UBS, I was spinning a web of lies. Consequences came with that irresponsible approach.

I began by lying to my family, trying to convince them I had left my career voluntarily. I lied to my closest friend and to everyone with whom I came in contact. Perhaps worst of all, I lied to the attorneys whom I had paid a substantial sum to represent me. Then I felt I had no alternative but to mislead government attorneys with lies when I took questions from them. My thoughts were that I could control the damage and since government attorneys were not questioning me under oath, I was not compelled to answer truthfully. I was wrong.

My ignorance of the law was not a valid excuse for the new felonies I created by lying to federal law enforcement officers. Although I may not have been responding to questions under oath, and thus was not in danger of perjury charges, lying to law enforcement officers is a crime in and of itself. Such lies violate Title 18 of the United States Criminal Code, Statute 1001, exposing offenders to five years of imprisonment for each lie.

I didn't learn that information until far later than necessary. Equally as bad as lying to federal attorneys were my efforts to conspire with others to lie. When government investigators wanted to question one of my friends about my actions, I coached him on what to say. Those efforts to manipulate the government's case exposed me to additional criminal charges known as obstruction of justice.

We've all heard clichés of the Miranda warning. It requires law enforcement officers to recite that dreadful warning all Americans know. Those who hear the Miranda warning should know that anything they say to a law enforcement officer can and will be used against the individuals in a court of law. It's serious. An individual does not have to talk with a government attorney or law enforcement officer. But if that person chooses to talk at all, he ought to tell the truth. That gem of truism escaped me until it was too late. In federal prison, I met many others whose lies magnified their problems.

Besides further exposure to criminal sanctions, living a web of lies had undeniable biological effects on me. For two years I couldn't sleep without taking sleeping pills, which left me groggy the following day. I ate too much, smoked too much, felt irritable and paranoid. I played out every scenario in my mind except the one that made the most sense. The truth shall set you free.

My attorney was correct when he told me that I was late to the party. Had I accepted responsibility for the bad decisions I made at the outset, I would have assuaged my troubles with the criminal justice system. Likewise, however, I would have spared myself the anxiety and stress and expense that nearly ruined me as I was spinning that two-year web of lies. Many white-collar offenders I met in prison expressed the same sentiment.

Once I decided to come clean and cooperate, I felt a cathartic release, as if the truth about my criminally wrong indiscretions purged the anxieties that had been tormenting me for so long. Suddenly, those worries about what was going to happen didn't plague me. By speaking honestly about my culpability in the offense, I felt as if I were taking the first steps to climb out of the hole I had been digging for myself.

During the year that followed my guilty plea, I had to tell and retell my story. I had to speak with FBI agents, U.S. attorneys, and attorneys from the Securities and Exchange Commission. I had neglected my duties as a financial professional. Decisions I had made enabled Gilabert to perpetuate his fraud with the GLT Fund, and as a consequence, I aided and abetted the loss of millions for unsuspecting investors. Those were criminal actions, and speaking honestly about them began the process of redemption, of healing.

As part of the legal settlement, UBS forked over the money to make all investors whole. In an effort to demonstrate remorse for the consequences of my actions, I liquidated my individual retirement account to contribute

$100,000 to a restitution fund. That voluntary gesture of good faith brought me considerable benefit. Not only did it help clear my conscience, but it also persuaded my sentencing judge that I was sincere.

On the day of my sentencing, I learned that prosecutors were asking for a two-year prison term. I could have received five years had I elected to continue living the lie and force the government to prove its case through trial. To my welcome surprise, the judge took my cooperation into consideration, including the voluntary payment I made to the restitution fund; he imposed a term of 18 months.

Accepting a sanction that included a lengthy stint in prison took some time. Deep inside, I really couldn't believe that I was going to prison.

I didn't know anything about living in confinement. More than anything else, I think that living with the unknown was the worst. At least the 18-month sentence brought some finality. I knew the worst, and I knew my release would come at least six months sooner than the terms for which government prosecutors had been asking.

6
My Prison Coach

On 28 April 2008 Bureau of Prisons administrators instructed me to self-surrender to the Taft Federal Prison Camp. Self-surrendering was a courtesy and a privilege that the judge extended. Had he not found me cooperative and trustworthy, the judge could have ordered the federal marshals to take me into custody immediately upon sentencing.

As a prisoner, I later met men who were locked in federal detention centers long before they reported to prison. That experience, I learned from my conversations with others, brought an onslaught of stress. In federal lockup centers, prisoners of every classification served time together. More than eight out of ten prisoners in the lockup would not be eligible for camp placement, and many of the men had predatory tendencies. By giving me the option of self-surrendering to the prison camp where I would serve my sentence, the judge spared me the struggle of a federal detention center and allowed me the time to put my affairs in order before I began my journey through prison.

With the legal expenses, restitution payment, and lost income, my troubles with the law cost me well in excess of a million in hard dollars. Again, had I acted responsibly from the beginning, the consequences of my bad decisions would have been far less severe. Yet as a man who was about to serve a prison term, I had to let go of the past and prepare for the future as best I could.

Without a wife or children, I was free to lease my residence for the duration of my anticipated confinement. My mother agreed to care for my dog. I felt sure that I had made arrangements to preserve what remained of my financial assets while I paid my debt to society. I learned later that ancillary consequences accompanied my criminal activities. This news came too late for me to act decisively. I will explain those details below, according to the troubling order in which I received them.

Prior to self-surrendering, I called Taft prison to inquire what personal belongings administrators would allow me to bring. Hopes for my laptop, Blackberry, and cell phone were all dashed, as the officer with whom I spoke said I could only bring athletic shoes and toiletries. I later learned that the officer misled me, and I suspect he had motives for doing so.

Believing that I could carry in some gear, my friend Brad and I went to Nike Town. I was tipping the scales at 210, which bordered on obesity at 30 pounds above my ideal weight. Not knowing how my routine in prison would unfold, the one goal I set was to drop those excess pounds. I purchased a pair of Nike's best running shoes, a runner's watch and some apparel I intended to use regularly.

After leaving Nike Town, Brad and I drove over to Tito's Tacos, a landmark in Los Angeles. "You better get it all in now," Brad suggested. "Who knows what the food's going to be like in prison?" We gorged ourselves on greasy, but delicious orders of tacos, enchiladas, burritos and other Mexican dishes. Despite our gluttonous blowout at Tito's, we drove to Baskin Robbins and dropped $28 on various ice cream desserts. An observer would have thought that I was eating as if I had an imminent date with the electric chair.

When I drove over to my mother's house on the morning that I would self-surrender, I felt as strong as possible considering the circumstances.

Part of the reason for my equanimity came with the cleansing of my conscience that accompanied my acceptance of responsibility and guilty plea. Still, I could not underestimate the value that came through a serendipitous relationship orchestrated through a combination of stubbornness on my part and love from my mother.

A few months prior to sentencing, judicial complications were resulting in unexpected delay after delay. Those stressful times challenged me and I struggled. I wanted the procedure to end. I had pleaded guilty, and I wanted the sentence imposed so I could embark upon the next phase. The system did not place a high degree of importance on my wants as a defendant.

In my frustration, I kind of curled up, like a turtle retracting into its shell. I didn't want to talk to anyone. I didn't want to entertain questions to which I did not know the answers. I just wanted to vegetate, alone with my double cheeseburgers, my cigarettes, and my online chess games. I quit returning phone calls, and I froze out all of those who loved me.

My retreat drove my mother to the brink. She searched the Internet for solutions or assistance, Googling information on white-collar crime, prison, or any keyword that might lead to the information she craved. She was a frantic mother, crying out for help, and she found a friend in Walt Pavlo, at EtikaLLC.com.

Walt had been an executive at the corporation formerly known as WorldCom. In that capacity, he became involved in a fraud within a fraud that resulted in his criminal conviction. Walt served a couple of years in prison, and while inside, he made substantive efforts to redeem himself through contributions to society. Walt published *Stolen Without a Gun* and launched a speaking career to contribute content on the subject of ethics. Through EtikaLLC, the company he founded, Walt spoke to tens of thousands, describing the flawed values that led to his demise, his experiences, and offered suggestions on how an emphasis on ethics contributes to success.

Walt's mission was not to serve as a prison consultant. Yet when my mother's search led to Walt's Web site, she explained her troubled state of mind, her worries over my fate and pleaded with him for guidance through an email. I was not talking with her about my case, so she looked for information wherever it was available.

Walt felt touched by my mother. He had been freed from prison for a few years, and to a large extent he had put that unpleasant portion of his life behind him. Although Walt had reached a level of success as an author and professional speaker on the international circuit, he was not immune to the pleas of a frantic mother's call for help.

In an effort to ease my mother's distress, he responded to the unsolicited email. My mother offered to pay Walt for his counsel, though Walt would not accept payment. He simply listened to her concern for my welfare, and then calmly, and confidently, walked her through every step of the process that I would endure. Walt assured my mother that I would emerge from the prison experience intact. The steady hand he provided during my mother's time of need was invaluable.

I received message after message from my mother urging me to contact Walt. She wanted me to learn from him to understand more of what was coming. I resisted her advice, however, as I was trapped in that funk where only solitude could comfort me. I did appreciate the help Walt offered my mother. In gratitude, I sent an email to thank him for helping my mom, yet maintained that I preferred not to discuss my predicament with anyone.

As he did with my mother, Walt responded. He indicated that he understood my mother's worry, as his parents had endured the same troubles. Essentially, Walt offered a glimpse of what was about to unfold for me. As a favor to my mom, he said he was available to talk should I ever feel the need.

In time, I did contact Walt. He had chosen to focus his career on public speaking though he also had a gift for individual consulting. Through many conversations, emails and one lengthy meeting, Walt empowered me to advance with confidence. He had made exceptional use of his prison time and inspired me to do the same. With Walt's guidance, I set goals I could achieve and really began to embrace the reality that I could climb out from the pit into which my bad decisions had sunk me.

7
Processed into Prison

On the morning of my self-surrender, I called Walt from my mother's house. I wanted to express appreciation for the help he gave my mother, and to thank him for the insight he had given me. That guidance truly made me feel as if I could handle the prison experience, and it helped me move forward from a position of strength. With that purpose, I could ease my mother's worries on our final morning together before my imprisonment.

I was not scheduled to surrender to the prison until two in the afternoon. From my conversations with Walt, I learned that reporting to prison earlier would lessen the possibility for complications. Prisons schedule a shift change in the late afternoon, and if I arrived too late, the possibility increased that officers would lock me in segregation for processing the following morning. Wanting to avoid the discomfort of segregation, I made arrangements to arrive well before noon.

My brother, Todd, met me at my mother's house, and together the three of us drove north on I-5 towards Bakersfield. We turned right off the highway and into the prison complex at Taft around ten. I steeled myself as my mother wiped away tears. We embraced and said our farewells outside, but Todd walked me in to the lobby of the administration building to ensure all would go well. When we saw an officer in uniform, I informed him that I was reporting to self-surrender, and I extended my hand to shake in greeting.

"No offense," the officer gave me a stern look, "but we don't shake hands with inmates."

When the officer refused my friendly gesture of a handshake, I looked at my brother. I knew my life had changed, at least for a while. I would have to embrace the reality that in surrendering my freedom, I simultaneously had to surrender some expectations of common decency.

As my brother walked away, the admitting officers asked for my name and registration number. I gave them my name, yet not knowing my registration number, I drew a blank. Understanding that I was new to the system, the officers asked for my birth date. When I answered, they responded by telling me that my registration number was 44499-112.

"Memorize that number," the officer told me. "You're going to need it."

I was then taken into custody. For the first time since my ordeal began, I felt the cold steel of handcuffs to my wrists. With my hands locked behind my back, I carried my bag of personal belongings as the officers escorted me through a series of steel gates and locked doors. By pushing buttons and signaling into surveillance cameras, officers in a remote control center would open and unlock the passageways that would lead me deeper into the prison.

We arrived at a processing center known as the R&D building or Receiving and Discharge. Once inside the locked center, the officers unlocked my handcuffs. They looked at the bag I was carrying.

"What goodies have you got there?" They looked at me with unrestrained contempt, as if I were a grown man carrying a bag for candy handouts on Halloween.

"These are my running shoes, toiletries and a few books. They're my personal items."

"You can't bring them in with you. Would you like to send the package home at your own expense, or do you want to donate them to the institution?"

Justin M. Paperny

"But I called here before. The officer who spoke to me said I could bring these items with me."

"Well, you can't. Do you want to send the items home at your own expense, or would you rather donate them to the institution?"

Feeling as if I had just been artfully robbed, I agreed to donate my belongings to the institution. I didn't know the real meaning behind donating my property to the institution, though I suspected I was likely donating my $200 running shoes and other belongings to some other cause, like the correctional officers wellness foundation. Either way, I had time to serve. I didn't want to create any waves, so I agreed to forfeit my belongings for the good of the cause.

Those who expect to self-surrender to prison ought to take that personal experience under advisement. I'd like to say it was unique to me, but while I served my 12 months, I made a point of interviewing and interacting with other prisoners. Some of those men had considerably more experience of living in prison than me, and by listening to their stories, I learned a great deal.

One lesson I learned was that, like I did, many white-collar offenders who self-surrendered called the prison before they reported. They wanted to inquire on what they could bring. Somehow, they all seemed to be advised that they would be allowed to carry some personal items in with them. When surrendering, however, after their family members had driven away, they were given the option of either donating the items or sending home the package.

The anecdotal lesson suggests that when a man self-surrenders to prison, he should not bring anything that he doesn't absolutely need. If he needs medication, he should bring the medicine in sealed containers with a letter from a physician. A health services representative of the prison will make a determination as to whether to allow the medication. Medications for heart ailments, diabetes or other biological issues will stand a better chance of allowance than sleeping pills.

Other items I've heard prisoners can carry inside include religious medals and wedding rings, provided the jewelry's monetary valuation does not exceed $100. Prisoners may bring currency or a U.S postal money order, as well, and administrators will post the funds to a debit account the inmate may access for commissary purchases. From what I'd been told, however, nothing else gets in.

After taking my belongings, the officers handed me a stack of forms. They led me to a cell of concrete and steel and locked me inside with a tiny, flexible pen.

"Fill out the forms," the officer told me. "Answer every question. Someone will come by to see you soon."

That was it, I thought. I was in prison. My friend, Walt, had prepared me with descriptions of what being locked in a cell would feel like. Those descriptions helped my anxiety. I knew the processing would take several hours, so I wasn't as antsy as I could have been. When I spoke with other white-collar offenders who self-surrendered, they said that they didn't know anything. They thought they may have had to serve the entire sentence in the locked room. I felt grateful that I at least had some forewarning of what to expect.

The forms were quite basic, inquiring about my medical needs and my psychological state of mind. The dense pages seemed to go on without end, requiring me to respond to hundreds of questions. After more than 30 minutes of reading the fine print, I finished. Then I waited. Alone. Locked in a concrete bunker with nothing but thoughts to accompany me.

Okay. I reasoned it was time to get started. I squatted on the concrete floor, kicked my legs back and began my pushup routine. I weighed more than 200 pounds coming in to the prison, and I was determined to embrace an exercise regimen that would ensure I left in better physical shape. I began in those first hours of my confinement. As I waited for the next round of admissions procedures, I was able to knock out six sets of pushups, with between ten and twelve reps each.

"Paperny!" An officer at the door called my name.

"Yes sir!"

"What's your number?"

"Pardon me?"

"Your number. Give me your number."

"Oh, I'm sorry. I've just come in. I don't remember."

"Date of birth?"

When I told the officer my birth date, it was as if I had given the open sesame command. He unlocked the steel door.

"Come with me," the officer said.

He led me through a maze of corridors and took me inside another room.

"I need you to strip naked. Throw all your clothes in the basket. I'll be back." The officer then walked out from the shell of a room. Feeling peculiar and somewhat violated, I took off my clothes.

I stood in that room, stark naked, for perhaps 15 minutes before the officer returned. He had a mouthful of chewing tobacco and he used a plastic Big Gulp cup from 7-Eleven as a spittoon. I didn't detect any emphasis on bedside manner as the correctional officer seemed to check me out. He was fully outfitted in a gray officer's uniform, with pant legs tucked into black jackboots. A black leather belt cinched around his prodigious belly, and the belt had numerous loops for all sorts of pens, handcuffs, clubs, and other artifacts that distinguish the profession of corrections. He wore a bright badge proudly on his chest.

"First time." He said it more as a statement than a question as he looked me up and down.

I felt as if I were a horse he was evaluating to purchase. By the look of contempt on his face, I didn't feel as if I was measuring up. Did he want to look at my teeth?

"Yes sir," I was deferential to his clear authority. "I've never been incarcerated before."

"Virgin, eh?"

"Excuse me?"

"Ah crap," the officer said. "It ain't nothing."

I didn't know what to do as he stood looking at me naked. It seemed to me as if an inordinate amount of time was passing. Finally, he picked up a white clipboard and clicked one of the many pens that he pulled from a loop in his belt.

"Let's get this rodeo started," he said. "Any tattoos?"

"No, sir. None."

The officer checked his clipboard. "Lift your arms."

I reached up with my palms forward as if surrendering.

"Lift your testicles," he told me.

I lowered my arms and complied with his request.

"Turn around," he said.

I gave the officer my back side.

"Bend over."

I bent at the waist as if I were trying to touch the floor without bending my knees.

"Spread 'em'."

I opened my legs wider.

63

Justin M. Paperny

"Not your legs," the officer barked, "your cheeks."

I felt as if he were purposely trying to humiliate me. Satisfied with what he saw, the officer told me to squat and cough.

"What?"

"You heard me. Squat and cough!"

After I forced a cough, the officer ordered me to lift my feet off the ground. Not understanding, I leaned to my right and lifted my left leg as if I were a sumo wrestler.

The officer laughed at me.

"Not like that. Let me see the soles of your feet."

The entire inspection ordeal felt humiliating. Apparently, I passed, however, as the officer threw me an orange jumpsuit and told me to dress. He then led me back to the cell where I had left my paperwork. The officer told me I could pay to mail home the personal clothes I had left behind, or I could donate them to the institution.

Finally, about four hours after I had self-surrendered, an officer handed me a pair of khaki, elastic-band pants and a white T-shirt. He issued me a pair of blue slip-on shoes and told me to change. This time no one stood over me watching. Once dressed, the officer brought me to a station for a photograph and fingerprinting. He then issued me an identification card and a handbook that listed the rules and regulations of the prison camp. That concluded my processing, the officer told me. He was ready to drive me over to the camp.

8
I Can't Believe I'm in Prison

The Federal Prison Camp at Taft was tucked away behind the fenced-in, low-security prison that served as the main institution. Whereas double fences that were wrapped and separated with coils of glistening razor wire surrounded the perimeter of the main institution, the minimum-security camp stood out in the open, unsecured by any physical boundaries.

I wasn't locked in any restraints as the officer drove me from the main institution to the camp. When he parked, I stepped out of the car and felt some relief with the first glimpse of my surroundings.

The prison camp did not bear any resemblance to the monolithic institution that had been clouding my imagination. Walt had told me that prison camps were pretty laid back, yet I had seen a lot of prisons depicted through films and television. I couldn't shake the images of an impenetrable fortress that would separate prisoners from society. The Taft Prison Camp, however, looked no more imposing than a corporate office park.

A carpet of lush green lawn, blooming flowers, and sprawling palm trees welcomed me as I walked into the camp's administration building. A friendly officer guided me toward the housing unit to which I was assigned, and I made my way to the unit designated with the address A4D.

The single building that housed the inmates was made of concrete, tilt-up construction. With long rows of mirrored, horizontal windows, the building resembled a headquarters for an upscale engineering firm. I arrived at the camp mid-afternoon, and I saw scores of other clean-cut

Justin M. Paperny

men in khaki trousers and T-shirts socializing as if they were at a country club luncheon.

I noticed a running track off to the side of the building, and I felt enthusiastic about beginning my exercise program. In my mind, I walked around with the intention of not talking to any other prisoners. Yet all around me, I found friendly people greeting me and trying to ease my lingering anxieties.

The long, two-story building contained four separate housing units, each with a capacity to hold approximately 150 men.

Taft Camp is unique within the Federal Bureau of Prisons, as a private company with a management contract presides over the facility. As such, it does not suffer the type of overcrowding that complicates life in other federal prisons. When I arrived at Taft Camp, the population in my housing unit was listed at only about 80 percent capacity, with 120 men.

I found the building quite spacious. As a youngster, when I traveled across the United States playing baseball, I frequently stayed in college dormitories. The housing unit at Taft reminded me somewhat of those college dorm rooms.

Inside, they were built for efficiency and yet I was surprised by how much open space was available. I saw four rows of cubicles that were rather sterile, each constructed of a cinder-block concrete. The floor was an unfinished concrete surface. The cubicles at the front of the dorm had one set of steel bunk beds and another steel rack for a third person. Two lockers were available for the prisoners assigned to the bunk beds, and the person on the third bed used a drawer and storage box for his belongings. A tiny writing surface with a swivel, backless stool was attached to the wall as well. I sucked it up and realized that I could get used to the living conditions. I expected worse.

The first place I wanted to check out inside the dorms was the bathroom facilities. As I expected, they were of the locker-room variety. Inmates in the dorm would have access to sufficient quantities of sinks, toilets, urinals and showers. The bathrooms were finished in tile and, considering how many people used them, they were remarkably clean.

As I took my introductory walk around the unit, I saw one large recreational room with three televisions mounted on the wall. The inmates listened to audio broadcasts through headphones. Tables were available for games, and other inmates were battling it out with a vigorous match of ping pong.

The unit had three additional television rooms, a room with four microwaves, an ice machine for inmate use, and a quiet room that some inmates were using to study.

As I was walking around, with a curious and disoriented look on my face, another inmate approached.

"You new?"

"Yes. I just self-surrendered."

"I'm David." He offered his hand in greeting.

I told him my name, and we engaged in some small talk. He asked where I was from, how much time I was serving, and whether I had ever been confined before. I found David friendly, and appreciated him taking the time to show me around. Then a question came that caught me a little off guard.

"Did you surrender with any money on your books?"

I didn't want to seem unappreciative, although I thought David was a little forward with his question. In my hesitation, he offered an explanation.

"I'm not trying to get all up in your business, but this is what I do. I've been in prison for a while and I've kind of got a little hustle going where I help the new guys settle in. If you want my help, I can get you some things to make your time a little easier here."

That was my first exposure to the prison hustle, the underground economy. It turns out that it thrives in prison, and just as it does anywhere else in America, money helps. I brought $343 with me upon self-surrendering, and I quickly learned that I would need more. I felt as if I were conversing with the character Red from *The Shawshank Redemption*; perhaps the greatest prison movie ever, but it was not an accurate portrayal of a minimum-security camp.

"What kind of things can you get?" I didn't know that I needed anything, but I was curious as to where David was going.

"I can hustle you a better mattress if you want," he began. "I also perform a lot of services. I cook. I clean cubicles. I wash clothes. I even iron and polish shoes. Whatever you need, I can help you with."

David, it turned out, was quite a hustler. He was serving time for a drug offense, but was supporting himself completely through work he performed for other prisoners. I took him up on his offer. Since I didn't know anything about prison, I probably should have exercised a bit more discretion and observed more operations at the camp before engaging in transactions with others.

Just before four in the afternoon, each of the inmates in the unit retreated to their cubicles. Administrators throughout the prison system scheduled a census count at that time. As I walked to my assigned cubicle, I had my first opportunity to meet the others with whom I would be sharing space.

Walking into my cubicle on that first day felt awkward. When I processed into the camp, the officer told me that I was assigned to the top bunk in cubicle 39. I hadn't seen another officer since. The camp felt as if it were a self-service prison. The other inmates lived on autopilot, knowing exactly where they were supposed to be and what they were supposed to be doing. When I walked into my cubicle, I saw a middle-aged man sitting cross-legged on his bunk as he read a paperback book by Stuart Woods. He looked up at me as I stood at the open entrance to the cubicle.

"Can I help you?" He seemed polite, a man of Asian extraction.

"I'm supposed to report to cubicle 39," I stammered, as I spoke, a little unsure of myself.

"Come in," the man stood to welcome me. "I'm Ted. Where are you from?" Ted was the second person to ask where I resided. People in the camp, I learned, were mostly from California, from both the northern and southern sections of the state. Ted was an engineer from Orange County, and within ten minutes I knew he was serving an 18-month sentence for tax evasion. He was cordial and helpful to me in understanding our responsibilities as inmates. As we were conversing, another man walked into the cubicle.

"Are you new?" The corpulent man in his fifties extended his hand in greeting.

"Yes," I responded in shaking his hand. "My name is Justin."

"Vladimir," he introduced himself and I detected a strong foreign accent.

"Where are you from?" I learned quickly that such a question must be acceptable in this new world of mine.

69

"Russia," Vladimir told me. I learned that he had been a professor of physics. As I was, Vladimir was serving time for fraud, though his sentence was 60 months. To me, that sounded like a lifetime, yet Vladimir was taking it in stride. It turned out that both his wife and son were serving time in separate prisons as they were convicted of participating in Vladimir's crime.

The housing unit became silent as an officer yelled that he was about to begin the count, a ritual that was scheduled several times each day. Ted and Vladimir explained that we were supposed to stand silently during the daily counts that took place each day at four in the afternoon and at half past ten each morning. The officers counted us at least four other times each day, yet during those counts we usually could remain seated or lying on our racks.

Following my first count, I noticed many of the other inmates in the unit swarmed into the corridor from their cubicles. It was like an immediate traffic jam, with men of all ages rushing to the television rooms, the microwave room, the laundry room, or toward the six televisions mounted against the wall. The movement brought an electrifying cacophony with hundreds of screaming conversations.

As Vladimir and Ted left the cubicle, I slumped in a chair, crestfallen and holding my head. The first hour was a bit dizzying and overwhelming.

Walt told me that I would get used to the prison as I adjusted, and that I shouldn't worry much in the beginning. Though I couldn't help myself, I uttered a mantra in my head that I was strong enough to make it through. Still, I couldn't stop thinking about 18 months. At that moment, a year and a half seemed like an eternity.

After an hour or so, I noticed that a quiet calmness had displaced the seeming storm of confusion in the housing unit. The change was rather abrupt. I emerged from my cubicle to see what had changed, and I found myself alone in the cavernous unit. The other prisoners had left the building and were walking toward the dining room, or chow hall as it was called.

I didn't have much of an appetite, so I walked outside toward the recreation area. I found the outside facilities reminiscent of high school. An oval track enclosed a softball field, a soccer field, and tennis and basketball courts. There were horseshoe pits, bocce ball courts, and bars for both dips and pull-ups.

A recreation building included several stepping machines, a treadmill, stationary bicycles and medicine balls for strength training. There were no weights available at Taft Camp, but clearly, those who wanted to focus their adjustment on physical fitness would have every opportunity. As I walked around the track alone, I renewed my commitment to work myself back into great physical shape during the time I would serve in prison.

After a few laps, I took a seat on one of the benches to observe. I watched men playing handball, tennis, basketball, and running. Others were engrossed in workouts on the bars. It felt as if I were in a public park, yet one with the noticeable absence of women, children, and pets. Again, I missed my dog, Honey.

Many were running laps, oblivious to their imprisonment. I wondered what the men had done to warrant a prison term, and I admired their sangfroid. Would I ever become so at ease? I still didn't know how I was going to make it through.

I thought about my mom, my dad, my brother and my sister-in-law. What were they doing? It was nearly six

71

o'clock and I had been incarcerated for less than eight hours, yet at that moment, I felt totally alone. Never mind that I was in the midst of hundreds of strangers; I missed my family. To take my mind off the self-pity, I stood and walked over to the library.

Bookshelves held thousands of books. I certainly had a selection that could bring me up to date on westerns, romance, mystery, thrillers, adventure, and science fiction novels. I didn't see as many nonfiction titles. Six typewriters were also available in an adjacent room with law books. I wondered how many people with law degrees were confined with me at Taft Camp.

Walking around and familiarizing myself with the new community settled my nerves. After more than one hour alone, I had had enough. I returned to my housing unit, feeling alienated, broken, crumbling from the weight of my imprisonment. David approached me again.

"You hungry?" he asked.

"Starving," I said, surprised and grateful that at least one person seemed to remember me.

"I thought you might be. I nuked some grub, saved you a batch."

"What?" I didn't understand the vernacular.

"I made you some food dude. Want it?"

"Sure, yeah, thanks a lot."

David brought me a plastic bowl filled with rice, beans, tuna, sliced tomatoes and onions. The food tasted delicious. As events would play out, that dish became a staple that would carry me through my entire prison journey.

"First one's on the house," David said. "If you want to ride in my car on the regular, you're gonna have to kick some in."

"What do you mean?"

72

"We need beans, rice, tuna," he explained. "I cook for a few guys. Everyone throws in some food and I do the cooking. Clean your own bowls. Want in?"

"Sure. How do I get you the food?"

"You're a real fish! If you've got money on your books, you can shop in the commissary. You can buy everything you need. Give me what I need on food nights, and I'll whip it up. I kind of have a menu. We do nachos on Fridays, pasta on Sundays, beans, rice and tuna all week."

I didn't know anything. David brought me a list of items that I could purchase from the store, known as the commissary. At Taft Camp we were allowed to shop twice each week, with shopping days assigned in accordance with the score our unit ranked during a weekly cleanliness competition between the housing units. In other prison camps, I heard that prisoners could only shop once each week.

David explained that as federal prisoners, we had to abide by a spending limit that would not allow us to spend more than $290 each month, exclusive of prepaid phone calls and postage. That limit sounded sufficient to me.

"Believe me dude, most guys burn through their limits quickly. If you have trouble keeping it legal, let me know. I can handle things for you."

"No, no." I said. "I don't want any problems. Had enough of those. I'm not interested in breaking the rules."

"Suit yourself. But if you need anything, and you will, remember that I'm the guy who can make things happen. I'll be by later tonight with your mattress."

I'd forgotten what David said earlier about the mattress. I felt too tired to inquire further, so I thanked him again for the meal and lay atop my rack to rest. I had had enough for one day.

The clock had not yet passed eight, and fluorescent lights were burning directly above my head. The unit was alive with prisoners relieving their stress with card games and seemingly tall tales from home. Amidst the chaos, I drifted into sleep.

That first night, I recall many dreams tormenting me. All I could think about was prison, apparently. One succubus after another, each a Venus with a head of flames, laughing and ridiculing me for the abstinence ahead. The cruel and unusual portion of my punishment had begun; denial of the flesh had become my reality.

9
Learning the Ropes

I was deep in sleep when I felt a tapping at my foot. I began stirring into consciousness, and I realized I was in prison. I knew I was on the top bunk. The tapping on my foot didn't seem logical. I kept my eyes closed, wanting to ignore it. More tapping, the feeling was undeniable. I lifted myself to look.

"Dude." David stood there whispering at the foot of my rack. He was speaking quietly so as not to wake the others in my cube. In the blackness of night, I couldn't register why he had awakened me. "Dude, wake up. I've got your mattress."

"What?" I felt groggy.

"I've got your mattress, Bud. Get up. We've got to make the exchange now while the guard's not around."

"No, no, I'm okay. I don't want any problems."

"Come on. It ain't nothing. One guy just went home. We're just going to exchange your mattress for his before somebody else does."

"What? What do you mean a guy went home? Why did he get to go home?"

"He went home because his time was up, Dude." David must have thought I was stupid. "Now, let's switch the mattress."

I climbed down from my rack, upset with myself that I had become drawn into a middle-of-the-night exchange with such a furtive feel. I didn't know enough about my new environment to be working through deals with prison hustlers.

After stripping off the blankets and sheets, I picked up the mattress. It was really more of a mat than a mattress.

The rack that served as my bed was a sheet-metal slab supported by four steel posts. A long rectangular mat of thin foam covered in vinyl functioned as the mattress. I folded the mat in half and carried it as I followed David to another cube.

He picked up the new mattress, and I stretched the mat I had been issued originally on the lower bunk. Then I walked with David back to my cubicle. I saw a clock with hands at the right angle of three o'clock; we were the only visible movement in the unit. I felt like a prowler.

David set the mattress on my rack and walked out of the cubicle. I climbed up after I hastily wrapped my sheets and blankets around me rather than the mattress, and as I lay down, I realized that David had made me an excellent trade. Whereas my previous mat had been so thin that I felt the creases in the sheet metal of the rack, the one he had exchanged for me felt two or three times as thick. Despite the minor anxiety that came with thinking I may have done something wrong, I slept better on the heavier mattress.

I slept so well that I didn't wake in time for the breakfast meal. The rigid schedule was a factor to which I would have to adjust. The morning meal began promptly at six, and in Taft Camp it concluded 20 minutes later. Those who were not in line by the time an officer locked the glass door leading into the chow hall went hungry.

With a growling belly, I began my first full day in prison. The laundry issued clothing to me in precise increments. My allotment included three pairs of trousers, three T-shirts, three pairs of socks, three pairs of underwear, and one pair of boots. I felt as if I were a soldier with all of the strict rules to follow.

I spent most of that first day waiting in lines. I waited interminably to see a nurse, a prison counselor, a staff member for the education department. After hours in the lines, a few superficial questions concluded my interview. The only meeting of any seeming relevance to me was with my prison counselor. Rather than dispensing any type of psychological counseling to cope with the blunt trauma of confinement, the counselor processed forms. Those forms would authorize my telephone and visiting access. The prison counselor also selected the prison job on which I would be required to work.

In federal prison, I learned, we could submit up to 30 telephone numbers that administrators would approve for us to call. The quantity was not too relevant, however, as we were allotted a limit of only 300 minutes per month. With an average of fewer than 10 minutes of phone time each day, I was forced to budget the calls by watching every minute.

To facilitate the possibility for visiting, the counselors issued several forms for me to send prospective visitors. The visitors were required to return the forms with personal information that the counselor would cross check with a criminal database. Provided the proposed visitor met the prison's criteria, my counselor would add the name to my list of approved visitors.

My counselor then scheduled me for an A&O seminar, which stood for Admissions and Orientation. She explained that I should watch for my name on the daily call out for when I needed to attend.

"What's a call out?" The counselor seemed to speak in a jargon that I didn't understand, though one that she expected me to know. I felt a little bizarre and a bit overwhelmed with all of the prison structures.

"The call out? Ask around. Read your inmate handbook. You'll get the hang of it."

The counselor summarily dismissed me. I felt responsible for learning everything about prison on my own. Fortunately, there were other inmates like David around who helped me get a feel for things.

I realized that I had forgotten about the inmate handbook that an officer had given me as I was processed in. I returned to my cubicle to find and read through the collection of stapled pages describing prison life in bureaucrat-speak.

Later, David introduced me to a few inmates. I struck a bond with Arthur, a graduate of UCLA who was one year into a seven-year sentence. Arthur had an urbane demeanor and style. He was tall and obviously devoted to exercise, as he looked as fit as an Olympic gymnast. Committed to working myself into good shape, I accepted Arthur's invitation to exercise with him.

The routine Arthur had set impressed me. Since he had begun serving his sentence, he lived as a model of discipline. Each morning he left his cubicle after the five o'clock census count had cleared. He sat alone at a table with his Webster's dictionary and thesaurus, and he worked on a manuscript he was writing about the crimes that led him to prison.

Arthur was assigned to work in the chow hall. His responsibilities required him to sweep and mop the dining room floor after each meal. Following the morning work session, Arthur returned to write more on his manuscript. He gathered his work together at eight to prepare for the first of his twice-daily workouts.

The morning session lasted for two hours. Arthur alternated a run of between eight and ten miles with a vigorous ride on the stationary bicycle. Following the cardio work, he devoted a minimum of 30 minutes to his abdominals. In the afternoon Arthur returned to the track for another 90 minutes of strength training. His routine varied multiple sets of pull-ups, dips, pushups, and extensive training with the medicine ball.

"A lot of guys have tried to work out with me," Arthur said. "The routine isn't for everyone. I haven't yet found anyone who could keep the pace day after day."

After my first day of exercising with Arthur, I understood why. He was relentless. The man was in his mid-forties, yet he pushed himself as if he were 20. Not having exercised more than the leisurely games of golf I enjoyed each week for the past several years, I felt exhausted when we finally finished the routine. I was determined to stick with him.

Later that day, in the early evening, I went outside for a stroll with David. He and I were not as compatible as I felt with Arthur, though in prison I could see that I would coexist with people from every strata of society.

Like many of the men in prison, David was serving time for a drug offense. He told me that he had begun experimenting with methamphetamine during his late teens, and the drug abuse led him into drug trafficking. When I met David, he was 25 and nearly complete with an eight-year sentence. As we walked around the track, I listened as David told me about the camp and what he had learned through prison.

"What's the story with that guy?" I was curious about a flamboyant prisoner who stood out like a neon sign on a dark night. All the other prisoners were wearing gray shorts and white T-shirts, but the man who caught my eye was wearing fluorescent orange shorts that were several sizes too small. He was middle aged, black, with a belly so big that his bright orange tank top could only cover halfway. The man wore his hair in the style of the 1970's Afro. He was short, yet he seemed to be coaching a group of hulking white athletes as they alternated on the pull-up bar. I couldn't help but hear his barking orders.

"Get your head up over those bars," the man yelled.

"Don't mind him," David said. "That's Big O."

"Big O?"

"His name is Oscar, but everyone I know just calls him Big O."

"What's he in here for?"

"There's a lot of rumors about that," David said. "He's supposed to be some kind of accountant from Orange County, probably pulling a few years for some funny paperwork or something. But word has spread around that he's some kind of pervert, likes to get squirrelly with the hog."

"You're joking right? A sex offender? I thought there weren't supposed to be any sex offenders or violent people in the camp."

"Like I said, the stories about Big O are only rumors. His paperwork probably says he's in for some kind of white-collar crime, but that don't tell the whole story. Lots of dudes serve time for selling weed or blow or whatever. They might never have no record for violence. That don't mean nothin' though. There's dudes walkin' round here who sure enough peeled some caps all the way down to the white meat."

"What do you mean, murderers?"

"No doubt. This may be a minimum-security camp, bro, but we're not all campers. Got guys in here serving massive sentences. They been in the pen, been around riots, everything. They just been in so long without any problems, or they're getting close enough to the end that they transferred down to the camp to chill out before release."

"That's good to know. Guess I better watch my step."

"You're cool, dude. It ain't nothin'. Long as you show respect to everyone, you'll skate through without a lick of problems."

"So like, has anyone ever been in prison for more than ten years?"

"Ten years? That ain't hardly nothin'. We got a grip a guys been down ten years. Now you start talking 15, that's some black-belt time. Got a few a them."

"People in here have been in prison for 15 years? That's a long time."

"Dead straight. See that dude on the elliptical machine?" David pointed to a guy who was exercising alone. He looked kind of oblivious to his surroundings. Kind of at ease in his own world.

"What's up with him?"

"That's the kingpin."

"What do you mean?"

"Word has it that he was some kind of coke lord back in the day. He's been down for more than 21 years. He's in our unit. They say he writes about prison."

"That's a lot of time," I said. "What's a guy like that doing in a camp? I didn't think I'd be around criminals like that. Could that be right, that he's been in prison for so long?" I was skeptical.

"For real. Dude's been down since the eighties. I ain't never talked to him, but he seems all right, kind of burnt out. Always writing, watching the stock market or exercising. You'll probably get to know him. Seems to only talk to white-collar types."

"What's his name?"

"That's Michael Santos. Dude's got a 45-year sentence."

10
The Kingpin

Over the days to follow, I settled into my own regular routine with Arthur. Each morning I joined him for breakfast. He disciplined himself with his diet as well as he disciplined himself with exercise. Arthur would limit his intake to black coffee, bran cereal or oatmeal in the morning. After our workout he ate a slice of whole-wheat bread with a thin layer of peanut butter for the protein. Then he would eat an apple. In the early evening, Arthur had a rapacious appetite for beans, brown rice and tuna. He would not touch chips, anything fried, or cheese. The man was fanatical about health and fitness.

Prison, I was learning, would bring me an opportunity to reevaluate the patterns of my life. With my childhood commitment to baseball, I grew up with an appreciation for the virtues of discipline, honor and a sense of ethics. As I matured, those values carried me through my college years at USC. Yet when I ended my baseball career, I lost sight of those values. Instead of thinking about how much I would have to invest in order to reach my highest potential, I started obsessing about making money.

As I was growing up, all I thought about was how I could make a better contribution to the team. I surrounded myself with friends who shared those same values. Before I slept at night, I'd begin thinking about what improvements I could make the following day. And when I played well on the field, I always felt as if the team as a unit had won the victory.

That attitude really began to wash away as I entered the brokerage industry. I still remember my cousin, Todd Goodman, advising me to continue my education through graduate school. That eagerness to begin earning an income clouded my judgment. As a consequence, I found myself taking every shortcut possible. I had no loyalty to the profession. My interests were not in the building of a sterling reputation as a man of integrity, balance and discipline. My interests did not extend beyond the size of my check. I had no problem compromising the principles of good character if I believed I could advance my income.

My role models included my friend Brad Fullmer and my brother Todd. They lived differently. As a professional athlete, Brad worked harder than anyone I knew. He didn't only focus on developing his fielding or hitting talents. Baseball was his life, so he worked exceptionally hard to develop his fitness. Brad ran hard, he lifted weights, and practiced and trained all year round to ensure that he could make the greatest contribution to his team.

My brother, Todd, worked equally as hard in developing the business he was taking over from our father, and in providing for his wife, Sunny. Together they intended to build a family, and Todd devoted himself to building an enduring prosperity. He worked 12-hour days at his store, and along with his wife, Sunny, Todd diversified by building a family empire of rental properties.

Both Brad and Todd understood a parable that has held true for centuries, and that I was reminded of in prison. As shown in the legendary race between the tortoise and the hare, slow and steady always won the race. Those who constantly worked to reach their highest potential, and remained true to a core set of values, never fell off course. The key to success came through an understanding of values in life, and staying relentless in a commitment to add value through daily pursuit of incremental goals.

As I spent time with Arthur, I saw a similar contentment. He had already spent his first year in prison, yet he wasn't involved in any nonsense. He knew what he wanted and he pursued his goals with a deliberate focus.

Television or table games were not a part of his day. His exclusive interest was in fitness and writing his memoir. To that end, he applied himself to exercise. He restricted his diet and he devoted several hours each day to writing and reading. Arthur was in bed before eight each evening, oblivious to the pandemonium of the housing unit.

Arthur became my first role model in prison. I admired his discipline. As I lay in my rack at night, I thought about how I could emerge after my prison journey had concluded. Ever since I had finished college, my focus had switched from the long-term values that led to victory to short-sighted pursuits of higher commissions. I lived a penny-wise and pound-foolish life. I remember Todd Goodman telling me in disgust, "You mean you left Bear Stearns for a lousy bonus check at UBS? There's a lot more to this profession than a quick buck."

Brad was the same way. When I once asked him why he trained so hard during the off-season, he answered without hesitation. "I'm a major leaguer. The team pays me well to be the best I can be. The fans pay to see excellence. I owe it to them to work hard all year round. That's what I do."

Role models showed me that looking at the long term would lead to success. My life had spun into chaos as a consequence of losing focus. It led to unhappiness in my career, an unhealthy lifestyle, and an abandonment of good ethical conduct. While serving my time in prison, I resolved myself to live a more principle, centered life.

Like Arthur, I intended to discipline myself with a direct commitment to exercise. I pledged that I would drop the weight that had bogged down my body and mind for so many years. Conversations with other prisoners helped me understand that with the accumulation of credits for good conduct and a few months of halfway house placement, I could expect to serve approximately 12 months of my 18-month sentence in prison. When I finished, I intended to leave as a better man then when I had begun. My first goal was to improve my physical fitness.

I was well into my first week of confinement when I walked into the large room with three televisions. The middle television was broadcasting CNBC, and I stood there for a few minutes during the late morning for a glimpse of the ticker. The man David had referred to as the kingpin was sitting in a chair beside me. "How you doing, bud?" I was surprised to hear him speak, and looked around to ensure he was speaking to me before I shook my head in greeting and said I was fine.

"Just come in?"

Why was the Kingpin talking to me, I wondered. I felt a bit guarded, though he seemed friendly enough. "Yes, I self-surrendered this past Monday."

"I've seen you around, figured you were new. Do you need anything to settle in?"

"No, no. Thanks for asking. I think I'm fine for now." Although both David and Arthur had helped me out by lending a few necessities until I could shop in the commissary, I remembered that my friend, Walt, had warned me about accepting favors from people I met in prison.

"My name is Michael Santos," he extended his hand in greeting as if we were colleagues of some sort. He didn't have the mannerisms I would have expected from a man who had been locked in prison for 21 years.

"Justin Paperny."

Justin M. Paperny

"How long are you going to be with us?"

"Not long. I'm serving 18 months."

"Eighteen months," he repeated. "You'll see that the time passes really fast here. The sentence will be over before you know it. In fact, I'll do the time with you."

Obviously, he could sense that I was just getting myself together, and he was trying to set me at ease. He asked if I traded stocks. When I told him that I had been a broker, Michael opened a conversation about the state of the market. He didn't sound like a man who had been in prison for decades. In fact, if he were wearing a suit and tie, I wouldn't have been able to distinguish him from any businessman I'd ever met.

Michael was surprisingly open with me, and his candor had a charm to it, disarming my suspicions with tact. He told me that he had been convicted in his early 20s for leading a group that distributed cocaine and that he had been working hard ever since to redeem those bad decisions. The conversation that began in that television room of Taft Camp continued throughout my stay in prison. Surprisingly, it launched a new focus and growth in my life.

Later that evening, I took a few laps around the track with Bob, an inmate who was responsible for leading the Jewish community at Taft Camp. Bob coordinated the Friday gatherings and also presided over a discussion group. I found many social-type activities in the camp. On Monday mornings a public speaking group held meetings in the visiting room. Inmates with knowledge on individualized subjects offered other classes or workshops to introduce topics like investing, real estate or Eastern meditations. Such diversions, I learned, could help inmates cope with their separation from family and community while simultaneously educating or entertaining themselves.

"Do you know this guy they call the Kingpin?" I asked Bob as we walked the oval track.

"I know who he is, we haven't ever spoken. He seems kind of standoffish, aloof."

"What do you think of him? I mean, I wasn't really expecting that I'd be serving time alongside real criminals. We spent a few hours talking today, and he seems like a normal guy."

"I don't buy it," Bob said. "I've read one of his books. The guy's been locked up since the 1980s and he served time in some of the toughest prisons. Think about it. A judge sentencing a kid in his early 20s to 45 years . . . doesn't happen. Miami background? Cocaine? I hear he's Cuban. Probably off'd some people. Maybe didn't do it himself, but couldn't you see him giving the order to have some guy clipped?"

My conversation with Bob shook me a bit. My experience had prepared me to interact with businessmen and professionals. I didn't know much about judging the character of men in prison. Yet I was assigned to live in a housing unit with 150 other felons. We'd be sharing the same showers and toilets, eating at the same tables, watching television broadcasts side by side. I would have to get along.

"Do you play chess?" Michael caught me as I was walking into one of the unit's quiet rooms where he was seated. He had a dictionary and a thesaurus open on the table and he appeared to be working alone.

"I do."

"Care to sit for a game?" He gestured to another table with a chess set on the surface. "I need a break. Been writing all day."

"Sure. I'll sit for a game."

"Have you played much chess?"

"While I was on bond waiting to come in, I played chess online for hours each day."

"Wish I could do that. The Internet wasn't in existence when I came in. I've never accessed the Web directly, but I've got a fairly active Web presence out there. I write about the prison experience for guys like you. Did you see any of my work before you came in?"

"No, I wasn't looking for any information about prison. I just figured I'd learn about it when I came in."

"That's a real challenge for me. I know that I have a lot of valuable information to help people who are struggling through the criminal justice system. I've been living in prisons for my entire adult life, and I write about the experience as if I'm an open book. It's tough for me to reach my audience from here."

Our chess game advanced well, though I felt as if I had the upper hand. During those months prior to my imprisonment, I withered away hundreds of hours playing chess on my computer. Still, I moved my pieces with tentativeness. Despite Michael's ease of conversation, Bob's theory that the guy may have had someone clipped kept me vigilant about the possibility that I was playing with some kind of master criminal.

"How do you post your writings on the Internet if you don't have access to the Web or computers?"

"I write the content out in longhand, then send it to my wife. She types and posts it for me."

"You've been in prison for 21 years and you're still married? How does that work out?"

"I haven't been married the whole time. My wife and I came together in 2002. We married in a prison visiting room." Michael told me his story while casually moving the chess pieces. I was already up a pawn and felt that I was close to stealing his bishop.

"How did you meet a woman who would marry you while you were in prison? I hope that's not too personal, but that hardly seems possible."

"Not at all. Prison has kind of become my life. I write about it and talk about it all the time. My wife's name is Carole. We went to school together from fifth grade through high school. After graduation we kind of lost touch. It wasn't until about 15 years later that she came back into my life. Carole read something about my work and that inspired her to write a letter. Her letter led to correspondence, and in time, a romance. I was incarcerated in New Jersey at the time and she moved in order to nurture our relationship through visits. We married in that prison's visiting room, and she's been moving around from prison town to prison town whenever administrators have transferred me."

I knew I had Michael beat in the chess match. But I felt intrigued with the story he was telling. The thought of a guy spending his life in prison while still managing to build a family and an Internet presence made it sound as if conquering the system wasn't anything at all. Still, he might not respond well to losing, I thought. I gave up a pawn to kind of even things out in the game.

"Why do administrators transfer guys from prison to prison?"

"There are all kinds of reasons. When Carole and I were married, I was being held in a low-security prison. Later, my security level dropped to minimum. With the new minimum-security classification, the administrators had to transfer me from inside the fences to a camp."

"Do you think they'll ever transfer me?"

"Your sentence is short, and like I told you before, the time is going to pass a lot faster than you think. You will likely serve your entire sentence here. The only reason administrators would transfer you would be if you got into some kind of trouble."

"Like what? What could happen that would lead to a transfer?"

"You could get into a fight with someone."

"Well, I suppose, but why would I get in a fight?"

"Come on," Michael smiled. "You're in prison. This may be a camp but anything can happen. Although you can control your own behavior, you can't control the way the others behave. We're sharing space with hundreds of guys, many of whom are high strung, not quite all there. They can't handle the stress. Maybe a guy called home and heard a man's voice. Maybe some guy's wife just dumped him, or a family member died, or his kid won't talk to him. Maybe he felt patronized by the system. Any number of things could make a guy lash out. Fights can sometimes begin without anyone expecting it. If anyone is caught fighting in the camp—and it doesn't matter how it begins—both guys get transferred unless there are special circumstances."

That was it. I decided right then that I was throwing the chess game. I made a move that I knew would result in the loss of my queen. I wasn't about to aggravate a guy who had been in prison for so long.

"Have you been in many fights during all the time you've served?"

"You might want to rethink that move, bud. If you advance that knight, I'm going to get your queen for free."

"Oh, you're right, my mistake. Your game."

"No, no. You're playing well, you're really ahead. Take the move back. Try something else."

"It's okay. The rules are the rules. I moved the piece already. We'll just let it play out. I can still play without my queen."

"You sure?"

"Yeah, go ahead." I may have been giving up the most powerful piece on the chessboard, but at least I wouldn't be feeding into any of the unexpected tension he was describing.

"To answer your question," Michael said as he continued with the game, "I haven't been in a single fight during all the years of my imprisonment. Not one."

"How did you manage to avoid them?"

"By understanding my environment. I knew that I was serving a long sentence, but I wasn't serving a life sentence. Someday these gates would open for me, and I wanted to ensure that I would feel ready for the challenges that would await me. I set clearly defined goals, and my commitment to achieve those goals required that I adjust in ways that would minimize my exposure to potential problems. I relied on that strategy from the beginning, and I continue to rely upon it today. Check."

Michael had pinned me with a pawn. I saw the move coming, but I feigned surprise. One more move, I knew, and he would mate me with his rook. "It's your game," I said, while tipping my king over.

"Do you want to play again?"

"Not now," I said. "I'd like to hear more about your experiences through prison, and the strategy that has guided you through so many years."

11
Road Runner. Beep Beep

After that first game, I began spending a lot of time at Taft Camp with Michael. Approximately 500 people were confined inside the boundaries, though I noticed there was kind of a buddy system to serving time. Each prisoner had a few others with whom he became close. They usually came together because of similar interests and proximity. Those who lived in the same housing unit could socialize, eat, and exercise together. Friendships eased the pain that came with separation from home.

Counselor Micks assigned my first job in the camp. She was not particularly interested with academic pedigree. Neither the diploma from Montclair Prep, the degree from USC, nor the professional licenses I had earned carried much weight in prison; lack of a GED does not disqualify anyone from a prison job. I had been hoping for one of the laid back jobs that would afford me time to read and focus on fitness. Instead, my counselor assigned me to work in the kitchen. An inmate "supervisor" issued me a vinyl apron and assigned me to the dish room, where I was instructed to wash pots and pans.

Inmate work details were part of the prison experience. Officially, rules stated that no single inmate would have power or authority over another inmate. In practical terms, however, a prison protocol existed.

Those prisoners with more seniority stood a little higher in the unofficial hierarchy. Understanding that reality could make life a little easier inside.

At Taft Camp, counselors typically assigned new inmates to work in the food service department. Those job assignments could mean working as a cook or a baker. Similarly, a kitchen job assignment could mean cleaning tables, serving the meals from behind a buffet counter, or working in the dish room. Jim, the inmate clerk, assigned specific job detail for each inmate.

Officially, Jim did not have authority over any other prisoner. As the clerk, however, he made life much easier for the staff members who presided over the kitchen operations. Jim had been incarcerated for longer than 12 years. He was an old-style convict, with hair that was thinning to near baldness on top, but long and in a ponytail in back. Understanding every aspect of the food services department, Jim kept all the paperwork in order. He prepared the inmate payroll, filed the paperwork for the fire, safety, and maintenance departments. He organized work schedules and relieved staff members of having to worry about whether everything was in compliance.

Why would Jim devote so much energy to his prison job? Pay scales were nominal, with inmates earning anywhere from between $10 to $100 per month. My experience, observations, and lessons that I learned from listening to others convinced me that Jim performed his job with gusto for another reason.

Serving time in prison could rob a man of his identity, and his dignity as well. Through meaningful work, however, an individual could displace that sense of sameness and empower himself. A prisoner who had served as much time as Jim could find work therapeutic. Work helped relieve the thought of all that was missing from home. Rather than focusing on a release date that might stretch months or years, or even decades into the future, the long-term prisoner could focus on the tasks at hand through work. For Jim, that meant ensuring the food services department at Taft Camp ran smoothly.

Justin M. Paperny

In Viktor Frankl's wonderful book, *Man's Search for Meaning*, I learned a little something about coping with difficult situations. Viktor Frankl had been a prisoner in Hitler's concentration camps, and he suffered unfathomable losses. He watched Nazi officers summarily execute his immediate family and Frankl never knew whether the Nazis would extinguish his own life. Despite the traumatic conditions, Frankl said that he learned something about people's mettle while serving time in the concentration camps. Namely, people could adjust to anything by embracing activities that brought meaning to one's life.

Although Jim was an inmate like any other, he had created a little niche for himself. In his position, he had an office, a desk, and a typewriter.

Since he controlled the job assignments within the kitchen, the inmates might try to ingratiate themselves or influence his decisions with commissary items. Bringing Jim an ice cream might ease the way to a preferred job assignment.

I knew nothing about the protocols of prison when I self-surrendered. By the time I was assigned to the food services department, things were different. My friend, Michael, had already told me a great deal about the options available. Those conversations helped guide some decisions that could have turned out badly.

After Jim assigned my vinyl apron, I slid off my sneakers to exchange them for a pair of rubber boots that were community property. The fellow who had finished his shift in the dish room handed the boots to me as he was putting his sneakers back on. I grabbed the boots with some trepidation, unsure of the sanitary implications. I relied on Michael's advice about prison. He told me that I should brace myself for some discomfort, as there were bound to be rules and customs that I was not going to like while I served my sentence. "Trojan up," he would tell me. As I was grabbing the boots, I told myself the same thing.

With my pants tucked into my rubber boots, and the vinyl apron hanging around my neck and down past my knees, I walked into the dish room. I saw a fellow with long hair, tattoos, a goatee, and perhaps three teeth in his mouth. He was another inmate, and I presumed that he was in charge. The man's appearance suggested that he was not quite stable. He was tall, well over six feet. With the apron, he looked as if he could have been a stand in for some horror movie; all he needed was a chainsaw or an ax.

"I'm Justin," I introduced myself. "I've been assigned to the dish room."

The man looked at me, as if he were not quite sure whether I was predator or prey.

"What's your name?" I hoped to ease the tension. Trojan up, I reminded myself.

"Road Runner. Beep Beep."

I laughed, unsure what the man meant. "What was your name?"

"Road Runner. Beep Beep."

"That's what you'd like me to call you?"

"Beep Beep."

"Is it Road Runner? Or Road Runner, Beep Beep?"

"Road Runner, Beep Beep."

I shook my head as if in acknowledgment, then set to work by burying my hands in the warm sudsy water. The meal had been a rice dish with chunks of chicken baked inside. We had a lot of stainless steel pans to wash.

I was getting the hang of it. Then, without provocation or forewarning, Road Runner, Beep Beep let out a scream.

"Five minutes," he shouted.

Justin M. Paperny

I didn't know what had happened. His holler caught me by surprise, as if a canon had just set off an explosion. I nearly jumped out of my boots. Yet, Road Runner, Beep Beep kept feeding his pans into the dishwasher. I looked at him as if for an explanation, though he seemed oblivious to my concern. After I realized that I was working in an environment of questionable stability, I simply went back to work. I knew that I had at least another hour's worth ahead. The next time Road Runner, Beep Beep let out another holler about five minutes for no reason, I felt good about my mastery in ignoring him.

After the shift, I returned to Jim's office so that I could exchange my high rubber boots for my sneakers. I pulled off my vinyl apron and hung it on the rack. Jim was deep in a philosophical conversation with another convict. The man was in his early 30s, yet he went by the name of Dopey. Like Road Runner, Beep Beep, Dopey didn't have much in the way of teeth.

He was quite firm in his opinions as he was expressing them to Jim.

"Look," Jim said to Dopey in a tone of conciliation, "I'm not saying this whole thing hasn't been blown out of proportion by the Jews. But the Holocaust did happen. I just question to what extent."

Let it go, I told myself. I was in prison. There were going to be uncomfortable encounters. People were going to make comments with which I would not agree. Racial and ethnic tensions might exist. The best strategy for powering through would sometimes require that I keep my mouth shut and move on. With my sneakers laced, I nodded to Jim and Dopey and walked back to D dorm.

12
Intro to Philosophy

Later that evening, Michael walked past my cubicle when I was stuck in the doldrums. For the most part, I was adjusting well to my first weeks in confinement. Sometimes, however, I looked at the calendar with trepidation. Another full year of imprisonment would have to pass, at the minimum, before accumulated good conduct time and halfway house placement would warrant my release to quasi freedom. During those moments, I slumped into my plastic chair, bent over at the waist and held my head in my hands while my knees supported my elbows. I stared at the unfinished concrete floor, as if paralyzed in thought.

"Chin up," Michael said. "I've got great news for you." He rested his hand on my shoulder.

"What's that?"

"We're another day closer to home." Michael laughed as if my 18-month sentence was one big joke. He walked into my cubicle and sat on a chair beside me. He kicked his feet up to rest on the steel post of my bed frame.

"What's troubling you, young fella?" Michael was in his mid-forties, just more than 11 years older than me. Despite the amount of time we were spending together, I could not fathom how he had made it through so many years in prison without bearing any telltale signs.

"How do you do this?"

"What's that?"

"Prison, man. All this time."

"Prison?" He joked. "What are you talking about? This isn't prison. This is camp. Embrace it."

"I know." I leaned back in my chair and scratched my head. "I'm trying. Sometimes it just gets to me." I told Michael about the frustration I felt with my first day on the job. He laughed as I told him about Road Runner, Beep Beep, the repeated hollering of 'five minutes' with no apparent logic, the two white supremacists arguing about the existence of the Holocaust. "You say I've got to Trojan up and I am. I'm just used to a different crowd."

"Of course you are." Thus began Michael's philosophical dispensations.

"Do you want to know how to thrive through prison?"

"Desperately."

"Notice I didn't ask whether you want to know how to survive prison. Anyone can survive prison. In fact, every year our country's prison system releases 650,000 people. They all survived prison. It's a pathetically small number of people, however, who can truly thrive through prison. I thrive. Do you want to know the secret?"

"Yes."

"The answers are the same as in life. Philosophers have written about the answers for centuries. You can find the secret in the wisdom of Aristotle and Sun Tzu. Do you remember reading anything about either of them?"

"I was a stockbroker, remember? A client would call, ask that I purchase 10,000 shares of Microsoft. I pushed a few buttons to fill the order. That was my career. Not a lot of need to think about Aristotle or, who was the other guy?"

"Sun Tzu. He was a military strategist, and he preserved his ideas through his book, *The Art of War*, a book he wrote that has been around for more than 2,000 years. You'd be surprised how readings in philosophy can prepare you to progress through difficult situations. The wisdom from centuries ago can help us through all of life's challenges. I'll bet it even could have made you a better stockbroker."

"Okay. So what's the profound message of Aristotle and Sun Tzu? Tell me what I should know about them. Give me the abbreviated version."

"Two points," Michael said. He held up his first finger. "Know thyself. That's a lesson from Aristotle." He held up his second finger. "Know thy enemy. A lesson from Sun Tzu."

I looked at him for a second, as if waiting for the punch line. "You're kidding me. That's the wisdom of the centuries? Are you serious?"

"Totally. One of Aristotle's famous quotes was that the unexamined life was not worth living. He suggested that for a man to reach his highest potential, he really had to understand himself, to know the values of his life. Only by knowing what was important to him, could he set a balanced strategy that would lead to his personal fulfillment."

"And the other one? What kind of cryptic advice did he give? I feel like I'm being given the ancient version of the fortune cookie."

"This fortune cookie quotes Sun Tzu as advising others to know thy enemy."

"So who's my enemy?"

"I don't think the enemy has to be a who. Maybe it's a what. Maybe it's a prison term. Maybe it's an unfulfilling career that leads you to misery, or to bad decisions that land you in prison. It's a treat for me to meet guys like you inside these boundaries. But I know you're not here by choice.

"Perhaps if you embrace the journey, you can learn something from it. Know yourself. Know your enemy."

Justin M. Paperny

"Like I said, I sold stocks. I don't know what you're talking about."

"Okay. Take today for example. You felt put off by some of your new colleagues, Road Runner and Dopey. You didn't like their version of conversation."

"That's right. I have a little trouble subordinating myself to a grown man who calls himself Road Runner, Beep Beep. And I'm not too keen on sharing space with guys who question whether Hitler killed six million Jews."

"But if you know yourself, and you know your enemy, why does it really matter what other people think or do? All that matters is you know where you're going, that you advance toward the values and goals you cite as being important to your life, to your fulfillment."

"That's what I did. I kept my mouth shut and moved on."

"Not really. You may have kept your mouth shut and moved on physically, but you're still carrying aggravation with you. It's bringing you down."

"So what am I supposed to do?"

"Let it go. Forget about it."

"Let it go? That's what I'm doing."

"Think back to when you were a broker," Michael suggested. "Do you remember the office, the trappings of success?"

"Do I ever."

"Probably wore a nice suit, kept an impressive office, receptionist, all that."

"That's right." I felt a degree of comfort come over me as I reminisced about my past success.

"What would you have done if Road Runner or Dopey presented themselves in your office?"

"I would have picked up the phone and called security."

100

"Exactly. The office towers of Century City were your world. That's where you felt you belonged. You had your own customs and culture there. Isn't that right?"

"You bet."

"Well, my friend, you need to keep your eye focused on returning to that world. Leave here stronger than when you came in, more prepared to find happiness and fulfillment in that world. You can do that a lot more peacefully if you accept that. Just as Century City is your world, prison is the world for guys like Road Runner and Dopey. Let them have it. Don't let their words or customs interfere with who you are or where you're going."

My discussion with Michael helped. He was right. Prison was only going to be a temporary blip in my life. Many of the people I met at Taft would always struggle with the criminal justice system, unemployment, and personal relationships. I met and interacted with people who lived mired in a kind of systemic poverty.

Alan, for example, lived a few cubicles away from me. His story brought home that prison was a place of concentrated hardship. The challenge for other white-collar prisoners and me was to persevere as best I could, to add to the lives of others when possible, and to avoid altercations at all costs. Michael's advice about understanding strengths and weaknesses, about knowing my environment and myself was poignant and insightful; it was not the type of guidance I would expect from a man who had served his entire adult life in prison.

Alan lived a life that, sadly, seemed more typical of the men I came to know in prison. He was 33, like me, and he was expecting release around the same time as I was going to be released to a halfway house. Alan had served five years at the time we met, although his time inside

101

prison boundaries and his life before arrest seemed more of a struggle than I could bear.

Alan had a look about him that told his life's story. His nose was crooked from having been broken numerous times. Scars from jagged edges marked his cheeks. He had a few missing teeth, and prior abuse of meth had rotted the teeth he had remaining in his mouth.

Alan's body was scrawny. Drawings of spider webs, skulls, and demons in bluish-green ink tattooed both of his arms. When I asked where he had gotten his tattoos, Alan told me that he had done most of them himself.

"We did it when we were kids in juvie." As we waited in one of the seemingly endless commissary lines, Alan opened up.

Troubles with the criminal justice system began for Alan when he was 13. He spent six months in juvenile hall on account of his having been caught shoplifting. Since then, he had been in and out of various institutions. Ordinarily, I would have said that Alan should have learned his lesson, gotten a job, put his life in order. Yet as I listened to the life he described, I felt a sense of empathy and became less judgmental than would have been the case had we not served time together.

During the most recent stint of Alan's imprisonment, his father had died in a car accident, his sister had been murdered, his mother had been incarcerated, and the mother of his seven-year old child had become addicted to meth. Alan was scheduled for release at the same time as I was scheduled to conclude my term. Whereas I would return to my place in Studio City, Alan had no idea where he would live or what kind of work he would pursue. He sounded lost and expressed little confidence in his ability to function in society. Prison had become the only world where he felt comfortable.

In listening to Alan, and the prisoners with whom I was confined, I realized that prison gave me an opportunity to become more tolerant of others. In one of the books I read, I came across the writings of John Dewey, who had been an influential educator from the University of Chicago. Dewey's work suggested that the bad man was the individual who, regardless of what good works he had done in the past, had ceased trying to make the world a better place. The good man, on the other hand, was the individual who, regardless of what bad he had done in the past, was striving to improve his own life as well as the lives of others.

In prison I had to live with guys like Road Runner, Dopey, Alan and others whose life stories differed in remarkable ways from mine. These people had not been blessed with the privileges that I had taken for granted. For such people, loving families, stable, comfortable surroundings, and career opportunities were abstract fantasies that they could not imagine themselves enjoying. Their lives had been one struggle after another, and an end to the turmoil did not seem in sight. By understanding the people around me, I empowered myself to endure what were really nothing more than the temporary inconveniences of my relatively brief stint in a federal prison camp.

Equally important, my exposure to others helped me understand some of the flaws that had contaminated my own character. Michael's brief lesson on the ancient philosophers Aristotle and Sun Tzu suggested that I must know myself and my enemies. I did not perceive that he meant enemies in the sense of other people who were out to ruin me. My battle was with a sense of entitlement that I had to conquer.

In loving and providing for me, my parents had removed the concept of struggle from my life. From my earliest memories, I believed that I had won the parent lottery as my childhood felt idyllic. Such a background eased my life, though it did not imbue me with the lasting virtues of good character, as my parents would have hoped.

Upon listening to the stories of the prisoners, I could understand how some of the men around me had made decisions that led them into troubles with the law. What excuse did I have? I was born with every advantage, and yet decisions I had made reduced me to the life of a prisoner. Aristotle's prescription for introspection would help me understand the motivations that drove me and how to prepare for a better life ahead.

Had I embraced the concept of knowing myself and knowing my enemies as I ventured into the professional world, perhaps I would have lived more responsibly. Upon my first encounter with struggles as a stockbroker, I began taking short cuts. Rather than pursuing lasting success as my cousin, Todd Goodman, observed, I chased the temptations of quick and easy commissions. Cheating became easy to rationalize, as I felt entitled to more.

As I served my sentence in Taft Camp, I came across an article in a business newspaper that described the work of Jim Ratley, a consultant who spoke on the motivations for fraud. Mr. Ratley said that perpetrators need to be in a position where they can commit fraud, they need the money, and they must be able to rationalize their crime. It was his way of describing the fraud triangle of opportunity, pressure, and rationalization. I should have known better. The more I thought about the motivations that drove my decisions, the more catharsis I felt come over me. I felt a cleansing, as if taking the steps I needed to become whole again. I had fallen off course early in my career.

While in pursuit of the next big commission, I had allowed my values to fall askew. Only in realizing, acknowledging, and owning such flaws in my character could I let them go and find strength to heal. The alternative would have been to cling to a negativity that seemed to prohibit growth for many of the prisoners around me.

13
Visiting

During those first several months of my sentence, I kept up with my friend Arthur's formidable exercise regimen. His discipline and total commitment to fitness really inspired me.

Each morning we ran or rode the stationary bicycle for 90 minutes. We followed the cardio routine with 30 minutes of abdominal work. In the afternoon we returned for at least one hour of strength training. Taft Camp did not have weight training equipment, though pull-ups, dips, pushups, and work with exercise balls sufficiently transformed my physique.

With between three and four hours of exercise, seven days a week, I felt as if I were really making progress. I shed more than 25 pounds relatively quickly while simultaneously picking up speed, endurance, and strength. During my first weeks in the camp, I played in a tennis tournament, but other than that week-end event, I did not engage in any organized sports. I was all about the tangible results of personal training.

As a man in prison, I think I needed those clearly-defined goals. Many of the men with whom I served time in the camp found exercise therapeutic. While pursuing our professional careers, we had neglected our health. In time, our bodies and fitness levels deteriorated. Rather than investing the necessary energy to stay in shape, we procrastinated or accepted our growing waist sizes as an inevitable by-product of aging.

In prison, people sought to correct years of neglect through rigorous exercise regimens. I knew several men who lost in excess of 100 pounds by regularly walking and dieting. The separation from society, and clearly defined release dates, motivated many to work toward better health.

Thriving through confinement had the same meaning as thriving through life. When we as individuals understood our lives, understood where we wanted to go, we could set plans in motion to assure success as we defined it. We simply had to know our environment, as well as our strengths and weaknesses.

Determined to realize some individual gains first, I asked my family and friends not to visit until I had served six solid weeks. I was writing home frequently, easing their concerns by assuring them that I was adjusting well. My friend, Walt, the speaker on ethics, who had served time before, had written a few timely letters that buoyed my spirits at critical moments. I appreciated those assurances that the months would pass.

My mother and stepfather, Ken, drove north from Los Angeles to spend a Friday with me for our first visit. Visiting in the camp was like visiting in an airport waiting area, or small cafeteria. My mother and Ken checked in by presenting their identification at an officer's desk. The officer in charge would verify that visitors had been approved by checking names against the inmate's visitation list and then admit the guests into the visiting room.

Understandably, my mother was quite emotional about the trauma of visiting her youngest son in prison. She had never suffered what she considered the public humiliation of visiting in such a controlled atmosphere. Once she sat at the table, however, I think she was able to see that the camp was not an oppressive environment. Vending machines were available for snacks. Children were playing and affectionate with their fathers. Husbands and wives were bonding by holding hands. The visiting room was a place of ease.

After the officers had processed my mother and Ken, he called for me through an institutional intercom page. I felt enthusiastic, as if I were a child who had performed well in school and couldn't wait to show off his report card. My weight had dropped to college levels. I had quit smoking. I had made progress that those who loved me would notice.

We enjoyed a wonderful few hours together as I assured my family that I was well. Michael and Carole were visiting that day, so I was able to introduce my mother and Ken to a friend I had made inside. The visit eased my family's concern, as they were able to see that prison camp differed in remarkable ways from the stereotypical prison images portrayed through popular media.

Following our visit, however, officers gave me a stark, no nonsense reminder that I remained a prisoner. As our guests checked out of the visiting room, the other prisoners and I who had been visiting needed to wait for an officer to search us before we could return to the camp. The search required each inmate to strip naked for an inspection that would confirm we were not smuggling any contraband.

"What's all this about?" I asked Michael as we waited our turn for the search. Six weeks had passed since officers first admitted me to Taft Camp. For the most part, I had grown accustomed to the environment. I didn't appreciate the reminder of my imprisonment.

"Don't let the little things bother you. Strip searches are one of the inconveniences of prison. Expect that they can come at any time. As long as you know and abide by the rules, the inconveniences shouldn't disturb you any more than a fly buzzing around. This is all part of prison. Embrace it."

Michael's ease with prison seemed surreal. How could a person endure more than 20 years and walk through every indignity as if degradation like strip searches were normal? Taken as a whole, he had spent more of his conscious life in various prisons than he had known in normal society. In a sense, I suppose prison had become normal for him. I had a hard time reconciling the length of time he had served with his steady, purpose-driven demeanor.

"Do they strip search in all prisons?" I wondered if every prison operated the same.

"In camps, the wardens have discretion on whether officers strip search after each visit. Some strip search random inmates, some do pat downs, some don't search at all. Depends who is in charge. Here at Taft, everyone gets naked."

"How about in higher security? What's visiting like there?"

"Much more oppressive. In FCIs and USPs, the guards strip search inmates on the way in and on the way out. Several guards walk around the visiting room, and surveillance cameras record everything going on. There's considerably more tension, especially in higher security. One of the privileges of camp placement is that visiting is easier on the families."

"How so?"

"When your family comes to visit," Michael explained, "they drive in, park, and after a simple, friendly check in, they sit in a relatively stress-free environment."

"So how is it different in higher security?"

Michael laughed. "Visiting in some higher security prisons is like visiting a war zone."

"Come on."

"Compared to camp, that's no stretch. When I was in the penitentiary I didn't even want visits. The visits caused more stress."

"What was it like?"

"First of all, just approaching the prison was traumatic. Family members had to check in at the security tower, where guards were patrolling the prison with visible assault rifles. Then the visitors had to proceed through metal detectors and submit themselves to searches and degrading questions. Officers would wave some kind of drug detecting wand over their clothing. If the wand detected a residue of drugs, they would send the visitor away and remove the visitor from the inmate's list. Despite the wand's notorious inaccuracy, many people lost visiting privileges. If they sat in a taxi and got residue on their clothing, handled money with drug residue, anything, the dreaded wand would pick up the scent. Babies, old people, anyone could be denied visiting."

"Couldn't they appeal the decision or something?"

"In higher security, guards are much more suspicious of everyone. It's a much different environment from the camp. There is a zero-tolerance attitude, and that extends to family as well as prisoners. They are assigned seats. Inmates cannot walk around or leave their assigned chair without permission. Even to use the bathroom, the inmate must wait for a specific time, raise his hand for permission, and then use the toilet under a guard's direct supervision. It's dehumanizing, but you get used to that as well."

"That kind of place makes camp sound like Disneyland."

"Remember that. A lot of camp prisoners take the relaxed atmosphere for granted. They become comfortably numb and forget that they're serving time in a federal prison. Stupid decisions wake them up in a hurry. Once they get transferred out of the camp to a secure prison, they realize how good they had it in minimum security. By then, it's too late."

"But that doesn't happen too often, does it?" As we left the visiting area, our discussion continued about higher security.

"You've seen it, haven't you? Since you've been in the camp you've seen several guys taken away. First they went to SHU. They spent time locked up, and then they were transferred."

"What's SHU?"

"The Special Housing Unit, though there isn't anything special about it. It's like a concrete bunker, a self-contained cell where prisoners are locked inside for 24 hours a day. It's the punishment spot, kind of a jail within the prison, otherwise known as the hole."

"Does everyone who gets sent to the hole transfer to a higher security prison?"

"No. The staff uses an objective custody and classification schedule that determines each inmate's security level. That calculation takes into account such facts as the inmate's criminal background history and the adjustment record he has built in prison. Depending on the type and frequency of disciplinary infractions he received, he may suffer sanctions that can include the raising of his security and the loss of good time credits. Sometimes, disciplinary infractions can lead to transfers out of the camp, or even new criminal charges."

"Like fighting?"

"Fighting is only one example. There are as many ways to have problems in the camp as there are ways for a driver to have a traffic accident. People smuggle in cell phones, they drink alcohol, and they gamble on card games or sports. It's not as important to contemplate all the ways a guy can have problems. A guy gets more value from

111

thoughts and strategies that will help him emerge successfully. By knowing what he values and what he wants, any prisoner, regardless of where he is confined, can assure that every step he takes leads him closer."

14
The "U" Shaped Curve

By the conclusion of my third month, I was feeling much stronger about my adjustment. Friends and family were driving up to visit with regularity, my exercise routine was progressing, and I was even getting along with Road Runner and other diverse groups of my fellow inmates. I kept my eye on my release date, understanding that tolerating any inconveniences of prison lessened my chances of disrupting the smooth passage of time.

Whereas I had once been a prison neophyte, after three months I had completed more than 25 percent of my time inside. The novelty and trauma had worn off. I still had some nights when I woke and struggled with insomnia. With thoughts about home, my dog, and all that I missed, I couldn't fall back into sleep. A friend gave me a reading light and suggested that I make productive use of the time by reading. Prison was all about adapting. Regardless of what was going on inside or out, a successful prison experience required the will to adjust, to evaluate change and adjust.

Like millions of Americans, I had a lot changing in my world as I advanced through the summer months of 2008. The financial markets were crumbling, decimating the value of investments that I had worked hard to build since the start of my career. What distinguished my predicament as a prisoner from those who did not live with any restrictions, was the freedom to manage my accounts.

Prior to my self-surrendering, my friend Walt, warned me that prison administrators frowned upon inmates who had any active involvement with business decisions. He told me that in prison, officers monitored and recorded every conversation over the inmate telephone system. One of the many prohibited acts that could result in severe sanctions was using the telephone to conduct business transactions.

Forewarned of such information, I made preparations before self-surrendering that I thought would protect me. I transferred my equity portfolio into a managed account where I believed that my broker would use his professional judgment to make market decisions. I gave my business partner discretion and access to resources in order to manage my real estate interests. While I served my sentence, I expected all of my business affairs would move along without complication. Not so.

After a few months I received information from the major Wall Street brokerage house where my stock market accounts were entrusted. As a consequence of my felony conviction, a compliance officer notified my personal broker that I would have to close my accounts. When my broker explained that I was in prison and therefore incapable of making any changes, the compliance officer froze my account, prohibiting my broker from conducting transactions on my behalf. As a prisoner, I was stuck, utterly incapable of responding to the rapidly deteriorating market conditions.

Just as the equity market crumbled, my real estate investments took a dive. The credit crisis that paralyzed markets across the globe was much harder to navigate from within prison boundaries. Whereas I thought I had protected myself by giving discretion to others, falling asset values required that I raise cash in order to hold onto my positions. My imprisonment made me impotent to handle my own affairs.

I spoke with Harold, another white-collar offender with whom I was serving time. He had removed all possibility of financial stress prior to his self-surrender. Rather than deal with fluctuating markets, Harold told me that he had completely liquidated all of his financial investments soon after learning that he was embroiled in a struggle with the criminal justice system. "I had enough stress in my life," Harold said. "I didn't need to complicate matters by worrying about money as well." He had put all of his resources in government-secure bonds.

If I had a do-over, I would have taken better precautions to protect my resources. As a prisoner, I found that I lacked access to current information, and rules prohibited me from acting decisively. Although I could occasionally catch a glimpse of the CNBC ticker, telephone regulations and other institutional obstacles discouraged prisoners from managing their own affairs. Although individual circumstances varied, experience convinced me that Harold's approach of eliminating all possibilities of financial complications would serve incoming prisoners best.

While expressing my frustrations to Arthur, my friend and workout partner, he counseled that I ought not to worry about what was transpiring beyond prison boundaries. "You're a bright guy." He tried to mollify my anxieties about what I could face upon release. "There's nothing you can do from here, so it's best you just forget about the outside. Concentrate on making the most of this experience and don't worry about what you can't control."

Arthur served his time with total contentment, not a care in the world. His exercise regimen carried him through. He had a supercilious air, and I enjoyed the time we spent together. Yet I had second thoughts about his guidance when, during one of our evening conversations, he belittled another man's optimism about the possibility he found for employment upon release at a hamburger chain.

115

Justin M. Paperny

"You're a prisoner working at a job in the chow hall wiping down cooking grills as it is," I pointed out. "Wouldn't it be better to be outside working at McDonalds?"

"I only work here because I have to," Arthur said. "I couldn't bring myself to work in a place like this if I were free."

In prison, I noticed many people adjusted in ways to ease the pain of confinement. For Arthur and me, that meant a total devotion to exercise. Others forgot about all they were missing by immersing themselves in recreational activities like table games, television or hobby-craft projects. Far fewer numbers committed themselves voluntarily to education or independent study programs.

The prevailing idea, apparently, was to forget about the outside world entirely in order to make it through the prison term. I noticed a problem with such adjustment patterns when I listened to men express genuine fear as their release dates approached.

Edward was a typical example. He had been a real estate operator for many years. I say operator rather than real estate investor or broker, because the ventures he described seemed more like a scheme than a genuine business. As Edward described it to me, he led seminars through which he encouraged those in the audience to apply for government guaranteed housing loans. In exchange for assigning over full management discretion of the property, Edward guaranteed an attractive rate of return to those who signed up with his program.

When changing market conditions rendered Edward incapable of living up to his end of the bargain, massive defaults on the real estate loans ensued. Those defaults led to criminal investigations and charges against Edward for operating a Ponzi scheme. He pleaded guilty and served three years in prison.

I met Edward as he was approaching release. He told me that he dropped a considerable amount of weight while serving time through regular exercise and dieting. An avid sports fan, he also joined others in watching ESPN religiously. A wake-up call came for Edward, however, when he received written notification from the U.S. probation officer who would be supervising his release. Edward showed me the letter, which stated categorically that the conditions of his release expressly prohibited him from any type of employment related to sales or promotions.

"Up until the time I received that letter from my probation officer," Edward said, "I always intended to earn a living through sales. That's all I know how to do. Now I don't have any idea how I'm expected to earn a living."

As I listened to more and more people express anxieties about the obstacles awaiting their release, a pattern began to emerge. Regardless of whether a man served a sentence of one year or ten years, when the release date approached, a new kind of anxiety set in. My friend Michael described it as the U-shaped curve.

The U-shaped curve measured a man's path through confinement or adjustment. To understand the theory, Michael told me to think of society as being above the U and the prison community as being below the curve of the U. As man enters the criminal justice system, he begins descending through the U. He feels himself leaving society behind and anxieties plague him as he moves deeper into an unknown world. The man begins to adjust, and he grows more acclimated to the world of confinement. He falls into a routine of exercise, television, sports or recreational activities. By the time the man moves halfway through his sentence, he will have adjusted in ways that sets him at ease with the prison community, which lies below the metaphorical U.

In advancing through the halfway point of his sentence, the prisoner begins to experience those anxieties again. The comfort level dissipates because he is ascending the U, knowing that he soon will leave prison behind and return to society. Table games, recreational activities, and four-hour exercise days will cease. The time of rent payments, car payments, and stress over paychecks comes closer every day. As a prisoner's time moves beyond the halfway point, regardless of the length of his sentence, the theory of the U-shaped curve suggests that anxieties return.

As Michael and I were in his cubicle discussing these patterns one day, he asked me to rate my own adjustment. I had passed through the first 25 percent of my time in prison and felt pretty much at ease. I was running much longer distances and at a much faster pace. In fact, I felt proud that I was running faster than anyone in the camp. My strength had returned, and I knew that I had worked myself back into the best shape of my life. People were noticing.

"On a scale of one to ten, with ten being the highest, what level would you rate yourself with regard to the commitment you've made to fitness and getting yourself in shape?"

I leaned back in my chair, flexed my arms, and rubbed the developing six pack of my abdominals. "No question about it. I've been exercising as hard as I possibly could. I'd give myself a ten."

"I'd agree with you. But you're talking about Edward, who is finishing up a three-year term. He's scared to death about what he's going to face outside. How much thought have you given to where you're going to be when you reach that step? On the same scale of one to ten, what rating would you give yourself with regard to preparation for release?"

His second question deflated my pride as quickly as a pin popped a balloon. I scratched my head. "Wow. I guess I haven't thought about it enough. I'd have to rate myself pretty low. Probably a one."

"Bingo." That was the ah-ha moment Michael was trying to elicit. "People don't succeed by accident and they don't fail by accident. Even in prison, the decisions we make determine the opportunities that open. The sooner you start preparing to ascend the U, the more confident you will be when release comes."

"All I've been thinking about is exercise."

"That's right," Michael said. "You need to realize that no one is going to pay you outside for how many pull-ups you do or how fast you can run. The sooner you acknowledge this, the better off you will be in allocating your time in here."

"What do you think I should be doing?"

"Every man needs to decide that on his own. Stephen Covey, an author whose work I admire, suggests that leadership requires us to live proactive lives, that we begin with the end in mind, that we put first things first. You've got to know where you're going. Then you can ensure that every step you take is leading you in the right direction."

"I haven't even thought about it. For the past three years my life was crippled with legal problems. Since I've been in here, I've just been unwinding, getting myself together. I haven't given any thought to what I'm going to do once I'm out."

"Have you ever read Dante?"

"What?"

Justin M. Paperny

"The Divine Comedy," Michael said. "It's a trilogy that Dante wrote several hundred years ago."

I knew Michael liked to draw lessons from books he read. "What's it about?"

"Dante began his story as if he was a man walking through a forest. Three beasts were pursuing him, rapidly closing in. Those animals were symbolic, representing the vices of lust, greed, and ambition. They threatened to consume Dante and ruin his life. As Dante came to the end, with nowhere else to turn, he met the ghost of Virgil, a legendary Roman poet who lived more than a thousand years before Dante. Did you ever hear that story?"

"No. What's the point?"

"In Dante's epic poem, Virgil offered Dante a way out of the forest, a way to escape the three beasts of lust, greed, and ambition that threatened to consume him. The only catch, Virgil told him, was that Dante had to put himself through hell in order to prevail."

"What does that mean?"

"In that poem, Virgil agreed to escort Dante through the various circles or rings of hell. Virgil pointed out the people who were supposedly suffering through the inferno, though it was up to Dante to draw lessons from the journey that would help him avoid such a fate."

"I still don't get the message."

"The message suggests that you're at the edge of the forest buddy. I'm your Virgil, ready to escort you through the hell of prison. I can point out what others are doing to keep themselves in the struggle, but it's up to you to learn the lessons that will change your life. You've got to confront and conquer your own demons."

15
Introspection

Michael's lesson on Dante stuck with me. There were vices and flaws in my character that I had to work on. I served time in prison for deeper reasons than ignoring the tell-tale signs of fraud at the GLT Fund. I was not in control of my ambition. I lusted for more, and I allowed greed to cloud my judgment. Despite my knowing that Keith Gilabert was perpetuating a fraud, creating victims out of his trusting investors, I rationalized myself into believing that I wasn't doing anything wrong.

I began spending time alone, tormented with thoughts about how my life had gone astray. The time in prison camp wasn't so bad. I never felt threatened or abused. There were aspects of discomfort, but nothing more than I could handle, and confinement itself was far less stressful than I had imagined. I could adjust and assuage the longing for home with hard-driven exercise routines.

Once Michael pointed out that I had to confront the flawed motivations that led to my disgrace, I hit a turning point. I was not alone in having been a man whose vices led him into prison. Hundreds of men were walking the same track with me. They were educated professionals who led distinguished careers. I met several attorneys, money managers, brokers, and even a few doctors. The prison did not seem to discriminate against anyone. People of all social classes and socioeconomic backgrounds were serving time. Every day, newspapers reported of professionals who had been accused of wrongdoing.

At the same time Bernard Madoff's $50 billion fraud erupted, a distinguished white-glove lawyer, who ran a large law firm bearing his name, was locked in prison

Justin M. Paperny

for having set up a scheme to defraud his clients out of more than $300 million.

As a man from the educated and privileged class, I did not set out to become a criminal. Until my period of introspection, I couldn't even bring myself to accept that I was a felon. I had not held a gun to anyone's head. Such delusions appeased my conscience, though they did not lessen my culpability. I had had every advantage. And on some level, the abuse of my privilege rendered my actions as despicable as any other criminal.

To conquer my demons, I had to confront the pernicious influences of lust, ambition, and greed. That meant introspection and knowing oneself, as Aristotle taught. Through those valuable lessons, I could contemplate how I wanted to emerge from confinement.

As far as formal educational opportunities were concerned, administrators limited us. Prisoners could study in classes that would lead to high school equivalency certificates and independent programs that Taft Community College offered. Neither of those options interested me before I hit the turning point in my sentence. I had to advance deep into the U-pattern of my adjustment before I became convinced to prepare as effectively as possible for release. I only had nine months remaining to serve. If I had more time, I may have sought to advance my formal education through independent study, not through a community college but through a university that offered such options.

Those who lacked high school equivalency, however, were mandated to attend GED classes. An individual's level of success in the business world would not exempt him from the compulsory program in federal prison. All federal inmates qualified to earn a maximum of 54 days in good time each year. Those good days were issued each year automatically to inmates who avoided disciplinary infractions, provided the inmate either had a high school equivalency certificate, a diploma, or participated in the GED program.

Staff members relied on the Presentence Investigation Report to validate whether an inmate had earned a high school diploma. I met one inmate who had graduated from high school decades earlier. Since the PSI report did not verify the inmate's graduation, however, staff members required him to study through courses in math, English, and social studies in order to qualify for maximum amounts of good time credits.

Inmates who had higher levels of education and self-discipline could work toward earning university degrees. During Michael's term of imprisonment, he earned an undergraduate and a graduate degree. The option to advance formal academic credentials existed for those imbued with motivation and determination, though formal educational programs were not the only method to prepare for release.

Since I only had nine months remaining to serve, and I understood that my criminal conviction would prohibit me from working as a licensed securities professional, I thought about the career changes I would have to make. I made a personal commitment to choose daily activities that would prepare me for success. Under no circumstances did I want to conclude my sentence like Edward, or like so many other white-collar offenders with whom I served time. Anxieties about how they would earn a living paralyzed them as their release dates approached.

The economic crisis of 2008 deepened as we advanced through the summer months. Unemployment rates soared to unprecedented levels. As more Americans felt the squeeze of financial pressures, more professionals rationalized their way into exploiting opportunities to ease their personal economic struggles. White-collar crime rates were skyrocketing and the experiences I had of having gone through the system felt relevant.

I thought about how much my friend Walt had helped my mother when he eased her concerns during the troubling times before my sentence. He had added meaning to his life by using his experiences to teach others. Walt built a career by speaking with audiences about the importance of ethics and by helping others make better decisions. The thought of working to empower others appealed to me. During the remaining months I was scheduled to serve, I contemplated steps I would take to refine my communication skills. My goal became to add value to the lives of my fellow citizens.

One lesson I learned in prison was that adversity was a universal, human condition. We all faced it at one time or another. In my case, adversity came in the form of troubles with the criminal justice system. Other people faced adversity of a different nature. They may have struggled with obesity, alcoholism, depression, relationships, or personal financial complications.

As a prisoner, I lived in the midst of personal struggle. Like Walt, my challenge became to overcome, to help others make better decisions, and to convey strategies that would guide people to reach their fullest potential regardless of the adversity in their lives.

As a federal prisoner, I obviously lived with limitations. The sanction imposed required that I lived within the rules of the institution for the duration of my sentence. For many, those rules served as an excuse for apathy. Rather than preparing for the challenges certain to confront them upon release, many inmates accepted what I perceived to be a mistaken premise that they were helpless.

"There isn't anything I can do from here." That was the common refrain I heard from the it's-not-my-fault crowd, those who insisted that they shouldn't be in prison.

Certainly, prison brought limitations that people did not want to endure. Those who focused on what they could not accomplish missed opportunities to strengthen themselves. A cliché held that misery loved company, and in prison I was immersed in it. Inmates found a sense of therapy in complaining. They found solace in talk-radio programs spewing conspiracy theories, and they comforted themselves through sympathetic listeners who clung to explanations on reasons why outside forces precluded their success.

Thriving through the adversity of confinement would require that I transcend the limitations. Instead of focusing on what I could not achieve as a consequence of my conditions, I thought about what I could. Just as prison anchored people with restrictions, I found that it also offered some advantages.

Namely, prison offered time to look inward. The more I understood about my weaknesses, the more I could work on developing strengths. Through a deliberate course of action, I could make the absolute most of the nine months I had remaining to serve. During my first three months I rated myself a ten on the scale measuring my commitment to physical fitness. For the remainder of my term, I pledged to devote that same intensity to my total preparation for release.

In realizing that I wanted to model a career on Walt's example of turning a weakness into strength, I knew that developing my communication skills would help. I may not have been able to gauge market conditions or interact with prospective clients from prison, but through deliberate practice, I could train myself to use English more effectively. Regardless of what career opportunities would open upon my release, I understood that developing my vocabulary, along with my speaking and writing skills would require a conscious effort. I also mastered the federal prison system and the policies administrators use to manage institutions.

During the first four months of my sentence, I followed Arthur's pattern and countless other prisoners by devoting myself to exercise. I had been working out for up to four hours daily. With my new focus, I made the commitment to devote twice as much time to understanding words, sentences, and paragraphs.

As soon as the officers cleared the morning census count at five, I gathered my Oxford dictionary and the writing books my mother had sent me. I walked to a quiet room where I could sit at a table to work. I made the decision to write every day. Since I did not have a writing instructor, I began to learn the craft through independent study. My self-assigned project was to document the prison experience.

I didn't have access to a word processor. But like every other prisoner, I had access to Bic writing pens that I could purchase from the commissary and all the writing paper that I needed. In forcing myself to write about my observations, experiences, and interactions with others, I realized that writing was hard. It required discipline, and I kept at it, knowing that just as I could work myself into shape by exercising, I felt certain that deliberate practice would improve my writing skills.

I sent the work home to my mother. Writing about prison became therapeutic for me. For my mother, however, receiving daily descriptions brought her an understanding of the circumstances challenging my life. She felt comfort in receiving those tangible pieces of evidence each day that verified I was making the most of a bad situation. I wasn't wasting away a year of my life with excuses and conspiracy theories; the term was serving me.

In listening to my mother describe how the daily description eased her concerns, and knowing how much Walt's descriptions helped her before my confinement began, I decided to reach out by publishing my observations of prison life and the lessons I was learning through a daily blog at justinpaperny.com.

My motivation had two prongs. On the one hand, I wanted to contribute to the lives of others. Prior to my coming into the criminal justice system, I never thought about how it could ever influence my life. I was sheltered from the world of jails and prisons. As a consequence of my not having known anyone who had gone through the system, I didn't give it any more thought than I gave to the disease of leprosy. I believed it was bad, though something that would never touch me.

As the complications of my struggles immersed me into the turbulence of the criminal justice system, I came to know it intimately. By speaking with other white-collar offenders, I realized that they had been like me; totally oblivious to myriad ways that criminal proceedings and prison could influence their lives.

By writing about the lessons I learned from others, as well as my own observations and experiences, I felt as if I could make a meaningful contribution to society. Others might find value in my work, and perhaps it could help them make better decisions. I know that if I had had access to information earlier in my experience, I would have made decisions differently. Those forewarnings would have saved me hundreds of thousands of dollars and perhaps spared me criminal prosecution.

Justin M. Paperny

Besides wanting to help others through distributing my writing more widely, I felt that creating a daily blog would prepare me for the career I could pursue upon release. I admired Walt for the ways in which he was able to help others understand the importance of ethical behavior. Those in his audience had numerous theoretical textbooks they could rely upon to study such esoteric concepts as duty ethics taught through Kantian philosophy.

Walt brought those theories to life by describing how bad decisions he had made led to his being locked in a prison cell, to losing his family, and to all of the ramifications that follow criminal convictions. Students may learn lessons through debating the wisdom of John Stuart Mill, Jeremy Bentham, and other philosophers who discuss abstract theories of ethics. I know real life, modern-day examples make the concepts easier to digest.

The daily blog would document more than one man's journey through prison. I also would express what I learned from others. My hopes were that writing those entries would provide depth and breadth to my content. At one year, my time in prison would be substantial, but by talking with others I could learn and offer considerably more information about the prison experience. Michael had served more than 22 years in prisons of every security level, and I had access to hundreds of other prisoners who had gone through the system. Everyone had a story. In writing daily content for blog posts, I could create value with a digital library.

Not knowing much about the technology of blogging, and not having direct access to the Internet, I had to train myself through reading. I asked my mother to send several books that would educate me on the subject. This project, too, assisted my adjustment.

In serving a prison sentence, an individual had to condition himself to reality. The system would rip away autonomy that most Americans took for granted. Once in prison, rules and policies dictated when, how much, and what prisoners ate. Administrators would assign where inmates slept, and with whom they would share space. Rules determined how much time prisoners could spend visiting or communicating with family and friends. The rigid structures of confinement stifled prisoners, and those prisoners who adjusted poorly suffered from depression, anxiety, and feelings of being marginalized or irrelevant.

I remember when I first began serving my sentence. If I heard of someone being released, I felt a sense of sadness paralyze me. The other prisoner's good fortune made me realize how much more time I had to serve. There wasn't anything I could do to influence my release date. Because of that helplessness, I felt the full force of being a prisoner.

When I decided to begin focusing on the methodical plan to prepare for release, I raised my energy to a whole new level. Instead of allowing the system to control my life completely, the personal investment I made to improve my writing skills and to understand blogging brought the feeling that through my own efforts, I could determine success.

16
Writing to Connect

Since I could not access a computer, I co-opted my mother to build my blog. She worked together with a Web designer and they constructed a simple blog that would allow my mother to load my entries. With that joint effort, I felt as if I were really participating in the world. Prison boundaries may have confined my body, but through those daily blogs I was sending my thoughts out into the world. That interaction freed me, bringing back a sense of the humanity that prison had a tendency of ripping away.

By launching the daily blog, I set a clearly-defined goal. Simultaneously, I announced that goal to the world. Accordingly, I wasn't only a prisoner anymore. I felt as if I had accepted a responsibility, a duty, and others would hold me accountable. Whereas I had been working early to improve the craft of writing for my own edification before, by launching the blog and announcing that I would publish each day, I gave myself an obligation. Suddenly, I had relevance. Others were reading my work, and I welcomed that sense of connectivity. I wanted to recommend that strategy to others.

I felt my writing skills improve through the work, though I also valued the input I received. For one thing, my mother felt less anxious about my welfare because she was intimately involved with the blogging project. With the daily postings, however, I began to receive feedback from total strangers. Some were about to come into the system, and they appreciated the glimpse inside of what they would face. I've heard and experienced that the greatest fear of all was the fear of the unknown. My work would shed a beam of light on the obscure world of prison and remove some of that unknown that people fear.

Writing had never been a part of my life prior to confinement. The more I wrote, however, the more therapy I found in the practice. As I interviewed other prisoners to write their stories, I often listened with sadness. Many told me how their confinement contributed in the destruction of their family relationships. Danny, a fellow white-collar offender who had been married for 15 years was crushed because his wife was leaving him after his first year of three in confinement.

"Did you try to sustain or nurture the relationship through writing?" I asked.

"What's there to write about? I'm in prison. She didn't understand that I was living the same day over and over and over again. That's what ruined our marriage. She said she didn't feel connected to me anymore."

Danny suffered the fate of many prisoners I met. He felt helpless. I explained to him how forcing myself to write was helping me through prison, yet he insisted there wasn't anything to write about. To paraphrase a stanza from a popular poem, Danny couldn't see the forest because all the trees were blocking his vision.

There was a great deal that those who served time couldn't control. Prisoners who capitulated to the system, who completely surrendered to it, rendered themselves impotent. They seemed to set themselves up for further loss. As their release dates approached, they suffered even more. Any prisoner, who walked out of prison gates without a plan, or at least preparations for the obstacles and challenges ahead, subjected himself to a continuing cycle of hardship. I learned this reality from the countless people I interviewed, many of whom had returned to confinement after release from previous terms. Surprisingly, some of

Justin M. Paperny

those people were well-educated professionals who served time for white-collar crimes.

Jack, for example, was a prisoner I had met. One of his ventures went bad, and upon investigation by authorities, the Justice Department charged Jack with violating securities law. He was convicted and sentenced to three years.

I would have expected a well-educated professional like Jack to rebound from his legal setback. When I met him, he was serving a one-year term for having violated the conditions of his supervised release. Jack had a law degree. If anyone should have known how to overcome the obstacles wrought by confinement, it should have been him. Despite the advantage of his education, Jack's life was disrupted in a significant way for a second time. I was convinced that had he done more to prepare himself Jack would not have violated the conditions of his supervised release. The more stories I heard from others, the more convinced I became of the need to push myself with goals of increasing intensity.

By the time I had completed my sixth month in prison, I crossed the tipping point. That meant I had more prison time behind me than I would have ahead of me. I had learned a great deal about the prison experience by then. Much more, I learned lessons that would help me through the remainder of my life. Surprisingly, I began to realize and truly embrace the concept that even through adversity, we as human beings could empower and enable ourselves. The ways in which we chose to adjust would make all the difference.

My hopes were to pass along what I was learning. I felt such an opportunity when, as I was standing in the midst of a hundred other inmates waiting for mail distribution, I received a letter from a woman who identified herself as Jane. Jane wrote because of her deep concern for her son, Ron, who was locked in a detention center in Oklahoma. She didn't understand why her son was not in the type of camp that my blog entries described.

From her letter, I understood that Ron had been convicted of bankruptcy fraud. His sentencing judge had imposed a 15-month term and had granted Ron the privilege of self-surrendering to serve his sentence. Ron was a resident of Idaho, and the Bureau of Prisons had informed him that administrators had "designated" him to serve his sentence at Taft Camp in California. To save travel expenses Ron would have to pay, however, his attorney advised him that he could self-surrender to the federal marshals in Idaho, and the marshals would transport him to Taft Camp.

Ron accepted his attorney's misguided advice. On the day the judge ordered that Ron begin serving his sentence, Ron presented himself to the marshals in Idaho. He waited in a series of Idaho holding facilities for three weeks, being processed from one jail to another. He finally boarded a prisoner transport plane that flew him to Seattle. He was processed into the federal detention center near the Seattle airport and remained locked in a cell there for another three weeks. Then the marshals chained Ron up again, and he joined the prisoner-transport flight. He thought he was flying to California. Instead, after stops in several states, the plane landed in Oklahoma, at a federal transit center. The marshals booked Ron into the federal detention center at the Oklahoma airport. He had been locked in that detention center for two weeks when his mother's frantic search for information led her to my blog. She wrote in search of advice or guidance.

In self-surrendering to Taft Camp, I was fortunate to have avoided the indignities of being transported around the country through the prison transport system. Wanting to learn as much as possible about the prison system, I interviewed scores of my fellow prisoners. From them I learned a great deal. My research revealed that many of my fellow inmates had received advice from their attorneys that was similar to what Ron had heard. As a consequence of their self-surrendering to the marshal service rather than to their specific prison, they endured a much harder beginning to their prison journey than I encountered.

In transporting prisoners, I learned from speaking to others, the marshals do not make direct flights. Economy required them to transport thousands of prisoners each day in the most cost effective manner possible. They also must factor security into their decisions as more than 80 percent of the prisoners they transported would serve sentences inside prisons of higher security than camps.

Since the marshals did not have the time to distinguish which prisoners had been convicted of heinous, threatening crimes like murder, and which prisoners were convicted of bankruptcy fraud, the marshals treated every prisoner with the same security precautions. That meant each person was stripped searched at the beginning and end of each transport day. Each man stood for a mug shot and fingerprinting and processing at each stop of the transport day. When traveling, each prisoner's ankles were bound in steel shackles with walking chains. Another set of steel manacles bound each prisoner's wrists to a steel chain wrapped and locked around his waist. The entire journey challenged each prisoner's equanimity.

What Ron was experiencing, in allowing the marshals to transfer him, meant that he would arrive at Taft Camp on the marshals' schedule. They were following a protocol that allowed them to transport prisoners to various designations with various senses of urgency. Those who had pressing court dates took priority over those who had been sentenced and were looking to travel on the cheap to cushy prison camps. He could spend longer than three months in transit moving from one federal detention center to another before the marshals' logistics schedule would transfer his custody to the officials in Taft.

Upon gathering the information about the prisoner transport system, I responded to Jane and told her what I had learned. Three weeks after I wrote to her, a young man who had just arrived at Taft Camp sought me out. He introduced himself as Ron, and thanked me for having taken the time to write his mother. Although my letter could not change any of the immediate struggles Ron and his family were enduring, at least the forewarning of what was to come helped pull them through.

I really appreciated the genuine gratitude that Ron expressed. It reminded me of the experience my mother had had with Walt. Once an individual was targeted by the criminal justice system, it was as if a journey through a labyrinth had begun. Each individual would have to make a series of decisions, and each of those decisions would determine whether the journey was severe or relatively stress free. In having information about what was to come, people could proceed through the labyrinth with one eye open. And, as the aphorism held, in the land of the blind, the one-eyed man was king.

Walt's information had comforted my mother. I was pleased to learn from Ron that in writing Jane, I had alleviated his mother's anxiety as well. The energy I was investing in writing the daily blog, as things turned out, was not only bringing meaning into my life. I was also contributing to the lives of others. Somehow, such activities brought a sense of connectivity. It helped me realize that despite my imprisonment, I continued to share a common humanity with all.

In Greek mythology, as I recall, a goddess by the name of Pasiphae mated with a bull with which the goddess had fallen in love. Together, Pasiphae and the bull had an offspring; the creature was half bull, half man, and was known as the Minotaur. Since the Minotaur fed on human flesh, a craftsman named Daedalus built an incredibly intricate and complex labyrinth to confine the Minotaur. Still, the beast remained dangerous, a threat to all mankind.

Theseus, a legendary hero of ancient Athens, whom some believed to have been the son of the god Poseidon, sought to save mankind by killing the Minotaur. To succeed in slaying the beast, however, Theseus would have to undertake a dangerous journey. No one had ever escaped the labyrinth alive, according to Greek mythology. Yet Theseus could only come close enough to kill the Minotaur if he were to descend into the labyrinth, a maze so intricate that he would never find his way out.

Ariadne, however, who was the Minotaur's human half sister, gave Theseus a solution. She gave him a ball of thread, which he unraveled as he went into the labyrinth. After killing the Minotaur, Theseus followed the thread to lead his way out of the labyrinth.

In progressing through my prison journey, I read through a considerable amount of classical literature. Those stories of wanderings and struggles and odyssey helped me realize that I was not alone. For centuries, ever since man had been using words to memorialize life, adversity has been a constant. We all relied upon others to help us through, and in so doing, we advanced as a civilization.

With statistics showing that more than six out of every ten people who came into prison failed again upon release, I realized that the criminal justice system was like a modern-day version of that symbolic labyrinth from ancient Greek mythology. This system of so-called corrections had morphed into a Minotaur-like beast that fed on human flesh, rendering failures of all who proceeded through the labyrinth. Although I may not serve in the role of Theseus, who slew the beast, by writing about what I had learned from others, and describing my own experiences, I could provide the thread that others could follow to find their way home and emerge stronger than when they began the journey.

17
The Turning Point

I was down to my final five months in prison. Letters from people who had been reading my blog continued coming in. I continued my work of interviewing my fellow prisoners for news on how I could help those who were struggling through their own complications with the criminal justice system. I felt a sense of usefulness. The more I focused on a purposeful adjustment, the more I seemed to empower myself through confinement. Writing and connecting may not have been the solution for every prisoner. In my case, however, the more time I served, and the more I interacted with others, the more I realized how valuable clearly identifiable goals became.

Robert was another offender who served time for a white-collar crime. He had been a CEO of a retail chain and had enjoyed a degree of success through his long career in business. His 48-month journey through the prison system, however, was killing him with bitterness.

Robert was in his late 50s, and he was in his final years of confinement when we met. He served time as a consequence of convictions related to securities law. Nevertheless, he insisted he was not guilty, and that he did not belong in prison.

I did not have enough information to make any judgment with regard to Robert's guilt or innocence. In serving time with him, however, I could see that rancor and envy ate away at him like a cancer. He complained about injustice. He bickered with staff constantly and many officers disciplined him for infractions resulting in his loss of good time, privileges such as loss of telephone access and punishments that included frequent trips to segregation.

Robert's adjustment pattern made his journey through prison much more difficult than it needed to be. Each man chose how he would adjust to adversity, and the choices he made determined or influenced his peace of mind. Although Robert could not undo the legal procedures that resulted in his confinement, he alone made choices regarding how he would respond to the setback of imprisonment.

My observations and experiences convinced me that those who set clearly identifiable goals during confinement stood in the best position to buoy their spirits. Robert had considerable experience in the world. Many within the prison population would have appreciated opportunities to learn from him. He could have taught classes or he could have worked individually in a mentor capacity to help others who wanted to learn. Robert could have exercised or engaged in independent study programs. Myriad activities could have helped him through his term. Instead, he succumbed to the negativity and seemed to drown in his own misery.

I attributed my successful adjustment through confinement to will and determination. I made the choice to thrive. That choice required that I contemplate how I wanted to emerge from confinement, and what specifically I wanted to accomplish.

To ensure my final five months felt productive, I set the personal goal of writing and publishing a manuscript that would detail the lessons I had learned through prison. Considering the fact that I had never written for publication before, and that I had never before written anything more complex than a college term paper, I understood the goal would challenge my skills and my discipline. The project would serve two purposes, however, and I embraced each with enthusiasm.

On the one hand, writing about the lessons I learned through prison would help me convey a sense of hope to others. I distinctly remembered the sense of apathy that came over me as I was struggling through the initial stages of my troubles. I remembered the sleepless nights and the bad decisions I made as a consequence of my ignorance regarding the criminal justice system. By writing about what I had learned, I could make a meaningful contribution to society. Others who found the work might rely upon it as a sense of proof showing that unexpected trouble with the law did not necessarily have to translate into total personal destruction. In my case, confronting adversity helped to recalibrate my life and rejuvenate my spirit.

Writing the book would also serve me personally. In setting the goal, I would have to exercise discipline, as my release date was approaching rapidly. By investing several hours each day in writing, I felt convinced that I could finish a draft in time to convert the manuscript into a book before I walked out. If I were to succeed with such a goal, I would have tangible proof that even through the struggle of confinement, an individual could channel energy and overcome adversity.

By writing every day, I felt as if I were building a ladder that would lead me out of the depths of my struggle. That approach could be constant or proactive. Whereas prisoners like Robert saddled themselves with worries, complaints, and resentment, those who sought adjustment patterns that allowed them to control their own destinies, so to speak, empowered themselves.

By immersing myself in this writing project, I had much more enthusiasm to carry me through the final months of my sentence. Since I knew that I had 150 days remaining to serve, and I knew that I wanted to complete the manuscript long before I walked out, I woke earlier each morning. To reach my goal, I sat down to begin writing before four. In the solitude of a quiet room, with my pen in hand, I felt at peace, as if I were not in prison at all.

18
Ethics

One of the many wonderful books I read during the nearly 13 months I served in prison described strategies to advance executive careers. In *What Got You Here Won't Get You There*, a successful business coach wrote about the different skill sets executives had to develop in order to reach the highest levels of their profession. Aggressive, competitive instincts could contribute to a successful individual career in sales, though the executive who aspired to world-class leadership would have to motivate entire teams and ensure the enterprise reached, or preferably, exceeded its stated goals.

Many people who had to endure a prison term could benefit from that same advice. The strategies necessary to advance through the troubling first months should transition into strategies that would ensure the individual concluded his term in the strongest possible position. The sooner that transition took place, the more likely the individual would become to emerge successfully.

Arthur, Edward, Robert, and other prisoners with whom I served time never seemed to grasp this concept. To cope with confinement they devoted themselves to activities that would not have much of a relationship to the challenges that would await them upon release. Prisoners, I became convinced, had a duty to anticipate the challenges ahead. Those who made adjustments and developed skill sets that would facilitate the lives they intended to lead, positioned themselves for success.

Such advice had a sophomoric feel. In prison, however, few men appreciated the wisdom of it until they had advanced so far along into their sentences that they lacked the time to make meaningful and measurable changes. The activities that were filling their days at the end of the sentence had a remarkable resemblance to the activities that filled their days during the first weeks of their sentences.

I had been on that same course. Exercise consumed the early months. The running, the strength training, and the dieting kept me going. I kept a journal of each day's performance, of every meal I ate. Had I not had that fateful discussion with Michael about my level of commitment to preparation for release, I likely would have stayed in that mode. Such were the patterns that contributed to so much failure in prison.

My plans upon release did not include aspirations for any kind of career in professional athletics. Physical fitness would always represent an integral part of my life moving forward, though the four hours of daily training were disproportionate to the goals and plans of my future. I had to advance through several months of my term before I felt strong enough even to set meaningful goals and plans. Once I did, however, I felt as if I had opened a new adjustment pattern that would assure my success.

The career I previously had led as a professional in the financial services sector likely was over. It had come to an end because of the bad decisions I had made. The pursuit of short-term gratification resulted in the sacrifice or forfeiture of a personal code of ethics. As I watched the financial crisis of 2008 spread across the globe and the reports of law enforcement investigations into white-collar crime, I truly began to comprehend the severity and magnitude of this problem. Lessons I learned from prison, I knew could help. These lessons began with my deeper understanding of the corporate culture from which I came.

The professional culture in which I was groomed rewarded those of us who contributed the most to the firm's bottom line. At the brokerage house of UBS, the importance of ethics, integrity, and honesty purported to convey the corporate culture. Daily practices and compensation schedules, however, belied such platitudes. The giant financial services firms rewarded those who brought in the money, and as current events showed, corporate America was content to feign ignorance with regard to ethical noncompliance.

In my own case, my partner Kenny Sorosky and I had every reason to suspect that Keith Gilabert was perpetuating a fraud with his GLT Fund. The trading losses of that hedge fund were unsustainable, though he continued to raise new capital. When confronted with further evidence suggesting an on-going fraud, Kenny and I did not terminate the account or notify authorities. We had commission schedules to meet. Instead of complying with a supposed ethical code, we manufactured a letter that we hoped would provide us with plausible deniability. That way we could continue to rape the GLT Fund for commissions while Gilabert continued to defraud investors.

Our superiors at UBS understood that the letter we generated misrepresented our responsibility. The letter apprised clients of the GLT Fund that Keith Gilabert executed all trades at his own discretion. Further, the letter avowed that UBS did not accept any responsibility for performance. It blatantly contradicted the brokerage house's commitment to ethics and integrity.

Our superiors at the global banking giant did not chastise Kenny and me for generating the letter. Instead, they applauded us for our ingenuity in keeping the account alive. UBS wanted Kenny and me to milk the GLT Fund for every last penny in commissions and interest. No one sensed a duty to the higher call for ethics.

As events transpired, news reports made clear that Kenny and I were not alone in our misplaced values. At the same time, UBS was not alone as a corporate entity that tacitly encouraged the pursuit of short-term profits, consequences be damned. Lapses in ethical commitment lay at the heart of responsibility for the financial crisis that had crippled our economy. The more white-collar offenders I met in prison, the more clarity I had of this problem.

Bob was one acquaintance I had met who served five years as a consequence of his conviction. As I did, Bob graduated from a well-known university and embarked upon a business career that was filled with promise. Within a few years of graduating, he was earning a six-figure income by selling advertising. As the Internet became a more ubiquitous presence in society, Bob saw opportunity. He launched his own company, and within a few years of forming his company, Bob succeeded in raising capital and liquidity through an initial public offering.

As chairman and chief executive officer, Bob felt pressure to exceed analyst expectations for quarterly performance. Investors expected a report card every 90 days, and Wall Street had an insatiable appetite for growth. If Bob's company failed to deliver the numbers, investors would punish the stock. They would sell it off in massive quantities, causing millions in losses of market value.

During the technology bubble of the late 1990s, Bob explained that profits didn't matter as much as revenue growth. When reports came in that Bob's company was not going to meet revenue growth expectations, the chief financial officer suggested that Bob authorize a barter agreement with one of the company's suppliers. That strategy would allow both companies to meet Wall Street expectations. In not disclosing the barter agreement, however, both Bob and his CFO understood that they were misleading investors about the company's performance.

Bob authorized the barter agreement. The practice lasted for three consecutive quarters before Bob and the CFO agreed to resume reporting numbers that accurately reflected the company's hyperbolic growth. The stock performed well and years passed before anyone ever noticed the financial chicaneries.

An audit of the company's financial records, however, led to an investigation. Like many white-collar offenders, Bob continued a string of bad decisions as a consequence of living in denial. Following his conviction, his judge imposed a five-year sentence.

I learned a valuable lesson from Bob. He was a man who believed that he had a strong sense of core values. The pressure of living up to Wall Street expectations compelled him to go along with a plan for financial subterfuge.

Bob was not alone. Thousands of students graduated from business schools every year. I read the insightful work of Jana Schrenkler, a professor of business at Saint Mary's University. Through one of her articles on ethics, I read about the challenges professors faced in trying to educate future leaders on the importance of making values-based decisions.

Without personal examples to draw from, Professor Schrenkler found that many students would miss the message. They would have read stories about corporate rogues and scoundrels, yet those case studies would not tell the full story. Students would, understandably, ask such questions as "What were they thinking?" and "How could they let it get so bad?" Business school professors would not have the answers.

Then the students would graduate. They would embark upon careers with clear consciences and solid sets of core values. Once they entered the corporate culture, however, they would face conflict and ethical dilemmas. How would they respond? In time, they too would encounter pressures, which might come from an unsettling desire for promotion or recognition. Opportunities for advancement would present themselves. Would the professionals have the moral resolve to make values-based decisions?

As an enlightened society, we would like to believe that all American citizens understand the concepts of ethics and good citizenship. By opening any newspaper today, however, we read of people accused of criminal acts whom others believed to lead sterling lives. I was once one of those upstanding citizens. I desire to reconcile with society and prove worthy of such a reputation again. To that end, I want to share these lessons I've learned from prison. By providing these personal experiences, perhaps I could help others to epitomize the discipline and forthrightness necessary to resist temptations that could otherwise compromise their ethical code.

In learning from Bob, others, and from my own experiences, I knew that a giant chasm existed between a corporation's written code of ethics and the practices that prevailed within the corporate culture. As the founder and CEO of his company, Bob told me that he was instrumental in writing the ethical code. Besides that, the Sarbanes-Oxley Act required Bob to sign all financial reports in order to verify their veracity under penalty of imprisonment. Despite writing the ethical code, and requirements imposed by corporate reform legislation, Bob was one of the hundred white-collar offenders who walked the track with me inside a federal prison.

My own experiences with UBS and Bear Stearns were the same. A written code of ethics meant nothing if it was not followed. An ethical code started at the top and leaders had to communicate that ethical code throughout the organization. Most importantly, I learned that regardless of the corporate culture, if an individual made a commitment to embody personal honesty, integrity, respect for others and to live as an open-book, that individual would triumph over every ethical dilemma.

Ironically, I knew all of this growing up as an athlete in Encino. I saw these values in my parents, in my brother and in my closest friends. They began to slide as I entered the financial services sector, and I had to come to prison to learn them again. Unfortunately, I wasn't alone.

"What got you here won't get you there," as Marshall Goldsmith advised, turned out to be more than the title of a book. Although he was writing for executives who aspired to lead the world's largest corporations, the wisdom Mr. Goldsmith dispensed had relevance for every human being. My reflections led me to conclude that the metaphorical U that Michael described applied to more than just prison adjustment. The human experience necessitated that we all learn different lessons as we advanced through different stages in life.

One of the lessons all of those who walked the prison yard with me could use concerned the importance of making values-based decisions. What did that mean? The more I thought about it, the more I learned about values-based decisions from Professor Schrenkler's writings, and the more I considered what other former executives told me, the more I realized that those who relied upon a corporate written code of ethics to form their center found gray areas through which they could subvert the code.

In my case, Kenny and I generated the letter for GLT Fund investors to absolve UBS of liability, not to look out for the interests of clients. Our motivations were wrong, and everyone associated with the letters we generated, with the exception of the client, understood that the letter violated the spirit in every line of UBS's written code of ethics.

When we as individuals slid into the gray area, we simultaneously made ourselves more vulnerable to the pressures that could lead to decisions with the potential to tear our reputations, our careers, and our lives asunder. Character flaws brought my fellow prisoners and me through the turmoil of the criminal justice system. We may not have thought of ourselves as criminals, though weaknesses in our moral code and a willingness to descend further into the ethical gray areas, led us to succumb to the pressures.

When we made that descent, we exploited opportunities. We rationalized our decisions. Rather than leading in ways that were inherently right, and making decisions that were consistent with our duty to act ethically at all times, we embraced that ends-justified-the-means approach to every problem.

On account of us operating from narrow and personal rather than global perspectives, however, our so-called ends-justified-the-means approach to decisions was nothing more than excuses. We used them as a crutch to rationalize our crimes. I heard such excuses from many of the men with whom I served time. Those were the moral lapses that brought us inside prison fences, or that "got us here." What type of changes were necessary "to get us there" back to the right side of good citizenship?

I had this discussion with Mark, who was in his third year of a seven-year sentence as we walked around the track at Taft Camp. He was a mild-mannered man in his mid-fifties, not bitter about his imprisonment, though not willing to accept full responsibility for the underlying

Justin M. Paperny

reasons behind his incarceration. To me, his story sounded like a clear slide into an ethical gray area. It was a slide that an individual with a stronger sense of right and wrong would not have made.

Mark was a graduate of the University of Pennsylvania and had earned his MBA from the prestigious Wharton School of Business. Following his university years, he built a career working for a global construction company based in Southern California. Mark earned an excellent living as an executive with the firm, but an extra-marital affair led to his employment being terminated, and a divorce decree that decimated him financially.

With employment rates being high in the early 2000s, Mark did not find many companies who were willing to hire men in their 50s. He sublet an office and began accepting work as a consultant on construction and development projects. In that capacity, Mark met Gary, who leased an office in the same building. Gary represented himself as a real estate developer who built housing projects in emerging countries.

"I'm working on putting a project together in Nigeria," Gary told Mark. "Would you be interested in flying over to complete some feasibility studies and due diligence in Africa with me?"

Mark accepted Gary's offer. Gary had had a relationship with some government officials in Nigeria. The development would provide multi-family housing projects that a municipal government was going to subsidize. Gary's company, supposedly, was going to oversee the development. Mark flew over to gather data that he would rely upon to publish a report supporting the viability of the project.

While in Africa, Mark collected information from local contractors, from suppliers, from labor organizations,

150

and from government officials. He had all the data necessary that would allow him to write a detailed report that would estimate project costs, time lines for completion, and revenue streams. Gary paid Mark handsomely for the professional report, authenticated with Mark's gold-plated academic credentials.

With Mark's report in hand, Gary published a glossy brochure that described the government subsidized housing-project development in Nigeria. He used the brochure in a prospectus he was sending out to investors with expectations of raising capital. Gary's company offered investors a guaranteed rate of return that attracted millions of dollars. Unfortunately for the investors, Gary never had any intention of building housing projects in Nigeria.

Mark had been under the impression that Gary was paying him to perform services for a legitimate enterprise. He agreed to return to Nigeria several months later on Gary's behalf to undertake due diligence responsibilities for a second project. While gathering his data, however, Mark discovered that Gary's company had not made any progress on the first project. Mark knew that the first project had been completely funded and that the time line had long since scheduled it for occupancy. Not even the building permits, however, had been secured.

That discovery led Mark to conclude that Gary had not been forthright. Upon his return, Mark expressed his concerns to Gary. "I've paid you to perform the due diligence and write the reports," Gary responded to Mark's inquiries. "Why don't you leave the project analysis to me?"

Mark said that he was not comfortable with Gary's response. Yet Gary had already paid Mark tens of thousands of dollars for his services, and Mark was not in a position to refund the financial advance. He completed his report for the second project and accepted full payment. Though Mark told Gary that he would not undertake any additional assignments from Gary's company.

Gary said he was disappointed with Mark's decision, but that he did not want to part on bad terms. Gary handed Mark a cashier's check for $100,000 and told him the check was a bonus for a job well done.

"You don't owe me any money," Mark told Gary. "You've paid me in full."

"Consider it a severance agreement," Gary said. "Contrary to whatever conclusions you may have drawn, our company is doing some good things for the Nigerian people. I want you to know we appreciate the services you've rendered in having advanced the development."

Against his better judgment, Mark accepted Gary's check. He used those funds to begin rebuilding his life. Two years later, however, FBI agents arrested Gary for orchestrating a Ponzi scheme. He had used the glossy reports to dupe gullible investors. Over the course of the conspiracy, Gary raised more than $20 million. That money funded a lavish lifestyle for Gary and his Nigerian co-conspirators, though it did not fund a single housing project.

Each of the thousands of brochures that Gary had sent out featured a photograph of Mark and offered a bio that boasted of his credentials. When investigators inquired about Mark's involvement, he provided a candid history of how Gary had retained him to perform the due diligence. Mark even showed the agents the field notes he had taken to prepare his report.

"Yet there came a time when you suspected a fraud," the agents pressed Mark.

"I figured something was not right. That's why I stopped doing business with Gary."

"Then why did you accept the $100,000 payment?"

"He wanted to pay me a bonus. I accepted."

The agents didn't buy it. Investors had relied upon Mark's credentials as a form of validation for Gary's supposed development. Prosecutors charged that Mark had discovered the fraud. In not reporting it, he had not only allowed the fraud to ensnare many more victims, but the prosecutors charged that Mark had accepted a six-figure payment as hush money.

As Mark and I walked the track at Taft Camp, I sympathized with the seven-year sentence that he served. He insisted that he was not a part of Gary's Ponzi scheme. "The man had paid me for services rendered," Mark asserted. "I was not part of any fraud. When I suspected that something wasn't right, I ceased to have any association with Gary."

That may have been true, I acknowledged, but Mark did not have an excuse for accepting the $100,000 payment. His separation from Gary, therefore, was not complete. That acceptance of ill-gotten gains was the crime that resulted in Mark's imprisonment.

"If the guy wanted to pay me a bonus, then why should I turn him away?" Mark felt frustrated.

As a prisoner, I sympathized with Mark. As a man who was struggling to right his own ship, however, I knew that a commitment to a higher moral code would not allow a man to accept money that he believed to be tainted. That was the lesson I had to learn. It was the way I needed to live my life moving forward.

Making values-based decisions did not require any written moral code. All ethics required was for a man to ask a series of questions, to put all dilemmas to the moral test.

Would my decision mislead anyone or obscure truth? Could I justify my decision to my unborn child whom I wanted to consider me a man of honor? Would others judge my motivations and actions as being consistent with the concepts of integrity and of good citizenship?

In the past I had ignored such questions. Instead, I focused on what I thought was best for me, for my immediate profit. From that perspective, I could justify a lot, but I could not live as a good man. Even if I made decisions from a so-called gray area.

19
Moral Codes

Lawrence Kohlberg, a former Harvard Professor, became well known through his writings on moral development. According to Professor Kohlberg, each individual made decisions from one of six stages. The deciding factors determining an individual's stage of moral development hinged on the reason behind a choice more than the choice itself.

For example, most people have a familiarity with the early-American writings of Henry David Thoreau. Thoreau lived under the tutelage of Ralph Waldo Emerson, of New England, and achieved a great deal of fame for his book *On Walden's Pond*. In that book, Thoreau argued for the beauty of a minimalist life. Thoreau believed man should strive to live as one with nature, in harmony with the people and land around him.

According to Thoreau, man should not pursue an acquisitive life. By creating and hoarding and expanding, Thoreau felt convinced that man's rapacious and covetous and insatiable desires would lead to ruin. He personified his philosophy by building a small cabin and subsisting by taking nothing more from the surrounding land than what he needed to survive.

As an American, however, Thoreau had an obligation to pay taxes. Knowing that those taxes represented revenues the government would use to fund expansion and what he considered to be an unjust war, Thoreau refused to pay his taxes. Authorities responded by locking him in jail. By today's standards, others might judge Henry David Thoreau as a tax cheat.

Justin M. Paperny

Professor Kohlberg, on the other hand might have considered the underlying motivations and reasons behind Thoreau's decisions not to pay taxes. Thoreau revealed those motivations in the less well-known book, *Civil Disobedience*. One passage in that book described Thoreau's response to Emerson's question about what Thoreau was doing in jail.

The question, Thoreau answered his mentor's inquiry, was why wasn't Emerson in jail? Thoreau believed jail was the only place for a just man in an unjust society.

Thoreau did not support American aggression as manifested through its Spanish-American War. Rather than contributing tax dollars that the government would use to fund more expansion and kill more human beings in the insatiable pursuit of more tax dollars and power, Thoreau chose to object. He willingly paid the price personally by sitting in jail, and he made such a choice because Thoreau felt deeply that it was the right choice for our society.

Thoreau was thus making a values-based choice of the highest order. He stood proud of the choices he made, and invited the world to hold him accountable, to judge him. That was decision making from a very different premise than the premise I had used in my decisions as a stockbroker.

I met many people in prison who served time for tax evasion. As I listened to their stories, and the reasons behind their actions, I understood that the motivation driving their decisions were much more in line with selfishness than with the higher levels of moral reasoning that Thoreau embodied. Like I was, they were scheming to keep as many nickels on their side of the table. When caught, they sacrificed their reputation and their freedom.

Steve was serving a four-year sentence on account of his conviction for tax fraud. He had owned a chain of electrical supply stores. He was also a real estate investor. Steve owned apartment buildings and other rental units. When making modifications to those properties he owned, Steve used supplies from his own stores. Rather than pay the costs for those supplies out of his personal income, Steve declared the supplies as expense deductions from his corporate books. An audit exposed Steve's deliberate efforts to evade taxes, and prosecutors charged him with multiple felonies.

As I listened to Steve's story, I realized how many business owners operated in the same way. They begin with small compromises they used to fill their pockets. Owners of retail establishments made deals with customers to avoid sales tax. These people did not consider their actions criminal. Prosecutors, however, saw things differently.

Living according to a code of ethical behavior would mean that an individual never had to look over his shoulder or cover up behavior that could bring shame and criminal prosecution. White-collar offenders who felt certain that their decisions fell ethically short, into gray areas rather than violations of criminal codes, filled our nation's prison camps. Few could accept that they were felons.

Marty was one white-collar offender who struggled through his 20-month sentence of bankruptcy fraud. He and his wife had been collectors of what was known as Americana art. They purchased furniture, paintings, sculptures, jewelry, ceramics, and other museum quality pieces. They developed reputations among other collectors as having discerning eyes for value. Marty wrote regular columns for many art publications.

Besides collecting art, Marty worked as a corporate lawyer for a publicly traded business. In time, however, some decisions led Marty into financial difficulties. He and his wife were forced to file bankruptcy in order to protect themselves from creditors. In order to complete the legal process, Marty and his wife had to categorize and value all of their assets.

In submitting the list of assets that Marty and his wife owned, Marty chose to cite the prices he paid for various objects. Some of those objects had appreciated in value by significant amounts over the years that Marty and his wife owned them. Instead of identifying an eighteenth-century armoire of superior craftsmanship, Marty's form indicated that he owned a movable wardrobe cabinet of negligible value. Marty's form claimed ownership of a coffee table, not a claw-footed table that was hand carved from oak in the 1800s.

He was not lying when he identified valuables as furniture and paintings. An unsuspecting bankruptcy court trustee would accept receipts of Marty's purchases from decades before as benchmarks for their valuations. Marty was a professional collector, however, and he understood the true value of his holdings. The bankruptcy forms he submitted were therefore fraudulent. When the government brought criminal charges against Marty for bankruptcy fraud, the prosecutor also charged his wife as she had signed the forms as well.

Serving time in prison felt bad enough for any individual. Yet when criminal decisions ensnared loved ones as well, the pains of confinement could feel magnified. Marty was unable to talk with his wife. They needed to obtain permission from the prison administrators in order to communicate by mail. Obviously, they could not visit. While Marty served his sentence at Taft Camp, his wife served her term in a federal prison for women that was located in Texas.

As a lawyer, it would have seemed that Marty would have known the consequences of providing misleading information on an official government form. He clung to excuses that the information he provided was factually accurate. Marty had listed his assets and he had listed the amounts he had paid for them. Those numbers, however, understated the true market valuations. Although Marty could appease his conscience by claiming the violations an "ethical gray area," the dissembling violated the law and resulted in imprisonment for both Marty and his wife.

The truth was that during the more than 12-months I served inside the boundaries of Taft's Federal Prison Camp, I met and interacted with hundreds of white-collar offenders. Each had a reason to justify why he was in prison. Some claimed it was an overzealous prosecutor. Others, like Marty, adhered to stories that they had violated ethics and not the criminal laws. As a prisoner I knew that the only way to reconcile with society was to own my decisions. I felt a sense of cleansing by acknowledging that I alone was responsible for my troubles with the law.

During the months that preceded my incarceration, I really didn't grasp the empowering aspects that would come with a complete acceptance of responsibility. I reversed my course of steadfast denial that I had initially set upon when UBS fired me, but that was more of a legal decision than a true change of heart. In the beginning I told lies to attorneys, to my family and friends, even to myself. I couldn't bring myself to admit that I had made decisions that not only violated my code of ethics, but also the criminal law.

After failing that lie-detector test, my attorney convinced me to plead guilty and cooperate with the prosecution of my case. I agreed, and I answered all questions truthfully. I sat for hours with government attorneys answering questions. The underlying reasons behind my decisions, however, were to minimize my exposure to sanctions. I cashed in my retirement account and surrendered a $100,000 check to the government before sentencing, not because I felt a deep sense of remorse, but because my attorney advised that such a gesture would boost my standing during sentencing.

What Got You Here Won't Get You There. As I came to the conclusion of my time in prison, I kept thinking about the title of that book I read by Marshall Goldsmith. Just as I had made decisions as a stockbroker in a misguided effort to advance my career and my short-term personal income, when I was responding to the legal complications that threatened my future, my motivation was a pursuit of the least possible sanction.

Those months I served in prison brought me a different motivation. I didn't have any options or angles to play that would lower my sentence or reduce the financial sanctions that awaited me. The judge had sentenced me to a fixed term. I would serve that time in its entirety whether I lived in denial or whether I reflected on the motivations that drove me to prison. Ironically, on account of my having had nothing more to gain, I gained the most. Through listening to and learning from the men around me, as well as my own introspection, I learned lessons that I would value for the rest of my life.

A journey through prison would not be an elixir, but I knew that it prepared me for happiness and peace and tranquility in ways that nothing else could. On account of my experiences of living in confinement, I felt better prepared to resist the temptations of those three beasts of lust, greed, and ambition. I had traveled through my own rings of hell. And because of what I had learned, I knew that my decisions moving forward would pass the ethical test. They would be rooted in honesty and integrity. They would be respectful and show my respect for the dignity of others. Because of what I had learned, I could make values-based decisions moving forward and that would make all the difference.

My readings in prison exposed me to many philosophers, and I was awed at how the wisdom from centuries past remained relevant today. George Hegel's writings instructed us that those of us who didn't know our history were doomed to repeat it. Had I known more about the nature of man, perhaps I would have had more appreciation for the nefarious influences of lust, greed, and ambition.

I found hope in the timeless debate over human motivation encapsulated in the work of Thomas Hobbs and John Locke. Both men lived in the 17th century, and their work influenced the shaping of modern civilization. The work of Hobbs instructed us that man was a selfish beast by his very nature, and that laws were necessary to keep him in order. Locke, in his brilliant essay on human understanding, argued a contrary position. Locke insisted that man came into the world with a blank slate, or *tabula rasa*. He said that man was not inherently evil or good, but that our behavior had roots in what we had learned from our own experiences and perceptions.

I agreed more with Locke than with Hobbs. As a child, I was influenced by the good role models around me. Through sports, I learned and lived by the virtues of good citizenship. After graduating from USC, however, I moved in a different crowd. By immersing myself in the world of money management, I became exposed to values of a lower order. The potential threat of laws did not stop my slide into behavior that violated the laws of ethics and the

161

Justin M. Paperny

criminal code. As Locke had written more than 300 years before, I learned bad behavior from the environment in which I had submerged myself. The good news was that through lessons from prison, I armed myself with new knowledge. They would help others and me going forward. My challenge would be in helping others learn these lessons before they felt the pull of pressure, opportunity, and rationalization.

I wanted to make some kind of contribution to society and I felt convinced that I could add the most value serving as a guide to others. Michael had told me that story about Virgil educating Dante regarding the consequences of bad decisions. In Homer's famous story of Odysseus, I learned the instructional value that could live for centuries through the recording and telling of personal struggle.

The temptations that led me to prison were the same type of enticements that had been ruining or challenging human lives for centuries. Adversity could bring pain and suffering for us and for those who loved us. Through proper perspective, however, we could learn lessons. We could grow. We could share our experiences with others, and through such contributions, perhaps embolden others to face their own struggles with courage. By telling my story, I hoped to enable my listeners by providing a thread they could use to find their own way through the labyrinths of life.

My tale was not exceptional. I succumbed to the temptations of greed and short-sighted self-interest. That slide in ethics led to complications with the criminal law. A prosecution resulted in my serving one year in prison.

Although the struggles were unexceptional, they were not unusual. Our nation's prison system confined more than 2.4 million people. Many Americans tended to think of those in prison as being of criminogenic

162

backgrounds. As a prisoner, however, I learned the startling reality. Twenty percent of our nation's prisoners, or nearly half a million people, stood convicted of white-collar crimes.

Who were those white-collar offenders? They were doctors serving time for health care fraud. They were lawyers serving time for bankruptcy fraud. They were accountants serving time for tax fraud. They were financial professionals serving time for securities fraud. They were business executives serving time for bank fraud. They were politicians serving time for honest services fraud. In other words, they were educated people who knew better but succumbed to what others have called the fraud triangle. What was the message?

Moral crisis was part of the human condition. We constantly faced dilemmas. People who graduated from business schools, law schools, medical schools and other professional programs burst onto the scene with high aspirations, and all too frequently, six-figure debts. They too would face the pressures. In time they would have opportunities that would tempt and lure them, that would test their moral convictions. Through these efforts to share what I have learned, I hoped to arm them with strength to stay true to the righteous path, to make values-based decisions.

My work may help disillusion misperceptions shared by so many Americans. When I graduated from USC I never felt the need to learn about the criminal justice system. Prison experiences, I thought, would never be a part of my life. The other white-collar offenders with whom I walked the track at Taft Camp felt the same way. We were wrong, just as millions were wrong when they compromised their ethics under delusions that their class of social status would immune them from prosecution.

Justin M. Paperny

Besides offering preventable lessons, I could also offer advisory lessons. Despite good intentions, bad decisions or life circumstances sometimes led us into adversity. This was a universal, human condition. When such challenges came, I hoped that those with whom I shared these lessons could find confidence to power through. We may succumb to temptations, but time immemorial offered countless examples of our resilience. We could thrive through turmoil and emerge stronger from adversity.

The question was would people listen. Plato, the immortal philosopher, wrote about the challenge of conveying lessons to be drawn from human experience. In his classic book *The Republic*, Plato told his story known as "The Allegory of The Cave."

In that fable, Plato asked his audience to imagine a subterranean cave. A group of people had lived their entire lives in that cave. Not only were they confined to the cave, but Plato described their movements and perspectives being restricted because they had lived their entire existence fastened to a pole behind them.

As a consequence of their circumstance, the people in Plato's cave could not comprehend or fathom the fullness of life. They had nothing more than what they could learn from their limited perspectives. By only being able to look straight ahead, they misperceived shadows for reality. Reflections from bouncing light rays brought illusions that those in Plato's cave felt certain were authentic.

That life of limited perspective was all that the dwellers of Plato's cave knew until one of the inhabitants broke free. He climbed out from the cave and emerged into all the splendor of the world. For the first time, he saw more than the reflection of light. He felt the power of light itself, with the sun beaming upon him and illuminating all around him. Suddenly life was more than a collection of shadows that he saw projected on the wall. Instead, he saw and experienced life itself.

Upon his discovery, Plato's cave dweller returned to the subterranean chamber that had heretofore been his only world. He was eager to share the lessons that he had learned about the world, to help others exchange their illusions for the beauty of reality. Instead of embracing those lessons, however, Plato told us that the fellow cave dwellers rejected such descriptions.

People have a natural propensity, Plato's allegory instructs, to perceive the world in accordance with their own perspectives. Conveying lessons from human experience represented one of man's greatest challenges. That was why Hegel advised that we had a duty to record our histories. We had to do our best to instruct others in order to prevent the cycle of mistakes. What got you here won't get you there. I would do my part to enlighten others through the lessons I learned.

20
Perspectives

Another Greek myth tells the story of Sisyphus, a man condemned to Hades as a consequence of his misdeeds. For eternity, Sisyphus was required to roll a boulder up a hill. Each time he reached the top, the bolder rolled down again, requiring Sisyphus to start from the beginning.

Prison could, at times, feel like a similar punishment. Just when the adjustment feels as if it's working well, disaster can strike. The prisoner must pick himself up and begin again. That was the reason that preparations were so crucial.

In December of 2008, I was in my eighth month of confinement. By then I felt as if I really had my adjustment in order. I had gone through the rigorous physical training portion, made the transition, and fully invested myself in an all-consuming program that I knew would help me emerge stronger than when I began my term.

I was exercising daily, in doses that I expected to sustain for the rest of my life. I was reading at least one book a week. I was interviewing other prisoners to broaden my knowledge of the human experience. I was writing blogs each day and devoting several hours to the writing of this manuscript.

Only five full months of imprisonment awaited me. I felt as if I were as prepared as possible to advance through with deliberate purpose. I had set clear goals, time lines for completion, and felt as if I were the captain of my own ship, steering it through turbulent waters toward the bay of tranquility. Then, without forewarning, I received disastrous news from home. My beloved dog, Honey, had passed away.

The loss was surprisingly deep, magnified because I had not seen Honey for eight months, and because I looked forward with such eager anticipation to holding and playing with her upon my release. Some would think the pain within me was too much, or exaggerated. After all, I was a 33-year-old man, well-educated and somewhat accomplished. I was at an age when others had enjoyed marriages and children. Though I had neither. For nearly the past 14 years, Honey was the family that welcomed me home at night.

When I self-surrendered to the prison camp at Taft, I left Honey in the care of my mother. During my frequent calls home, my mother always assured me that Honey was well and missing me. She sent photographs of the dog regularly, and if rules had permitted, my mother would have brought Honey to visiting.

In the evening after our Friday visit on December 19th, I called home to ensure that my mother had returned safely. Upon hearing my mother's voice, I could sense that something was wrong.

"What is it?" I asked. "Is it Honey?"

My mother held the phone in silence, unable to add to the complications of my imprisonment.

"Did Honey die?"

My mother began to cry. At that moment, I knew that my world had irrevocably changed. Nothing would bring Honey back. While standing there, in the openness of my unit talking on a wall-mounted telephone, the emotions poured out of me. For that moment, I felt naked, helpless, and inconsolable.

I wanted solitude, to grieve alone. As a prisoner, however, a man must accept that privacy does not exist. I retired to my cubicle and climbed onto my rack, feeling both exhausted and drained. The night was difficult to pass

Justin M. Paperny

through. Unable to sleep, I had to pause from my grieving and consider perspective.

Despite the need I felt for comfort, I had a sentence to serve. I had made significant strides in my mental adjustment over the previous eight months, and I could not allow Honey's death to unnerve me. Adversity and difficulty and struggle were part of the human experience, and I could not allow myself to fall apart.

Prior to the growth I had made as a response to my imprisonment, I lacked a strong enough center to cope with difficulties. When I learned of my troubles with the criminal justice system, for example, I lied to others and refused to accept responsibility. Instead of acting responsibly, I sought solace through midnight runs for double cheeseburgers and marathon sessions of online chess. In prison, however, there were no escape routes to hide from loss.

I had and would always have a love for my dog. Yet I had to embrace that the passing of life represented a part of the journey through which I and all others were traveling. The circumstances of life did not stop simply because my imprisonment had removed me from daily interactions with my family and community. Struggles would continue to come, and as a well-adjusted man, I knew that I would have to confront them with dignity and strength.

Imprisonment was much harder on family members than it was on prisoners. We could adjust. Our family members and loved ones knew so little about our environment that they worried incessantly. As I lay on my rack during the evening that I had learned of Honey's death, I knew that my mother was worried about how I would react to the loss. I made a commitment that when I hopped down from my rack in the morning, I would memorialize my memory of Honey by writing a blog. Then I would walk around the track for a couple of hours until my mother would wake. At 10:00 a.m. I intended to call her and set her mind at ease about my well-being.

I had lost a dog. Honey had been my pet since I was in college. And I loved her dearly. Yet I was in prison with people who had suffered losses of a far greater magnitude. Men with whom I spoke told me sad stories of being abandoned, without warning, by wives and children. Others had to struggle through news that their homes were being foreclosed upon and their families were being evicted. Men who had been removed from their families through years of imprisonment had to confront the reality that they could not provide effective guidance to children who were succumbing to drugs, gangs or other improprieties that could bring detrimental consequences to their lives.

Some long-term prisoners had a method for coping. Frank, for example, had been incarcerated for 15 years. He suggested that the best way to serve time was to forget about the world beyond prison boundaries. Since there was nothing he could do to influence that world, all he wanted to know about was the world in which he lived. That strategy, he said, would help him escape the pain that came with inevitable losses on the outside.

Such an adjustment was too extreme. One of the philosophy anthologies I read referred to Aristotle's theory of the golden mean. I understood the theory to mean that in adjusting to life, Aristotle was advising us to find balance, perspective. We had to prepare for the best, yet simultaneously we had to embrace the reality that there would always be more struggle to come. Although the news of Honey's passing shook me at first, I felt as if my measured reaction demonstrated a new maturity or evolution. Instead of allowing personal challenges or the complexities of life to derail me completely, the lessons I had learned prepared me to respond appropriately. I felt more composure, more equanimity, more capable of evening out the vicissitudes of life. Besides grieving for my own loss, I empathized with my mother and took affirmative steps to ease her anxieties.

One month later I was hit with more news from the "real world." Though it was of less momentous importance than Honey's passing, a message from home threatened my stability. As a consequence of my criminal conviction, I received notice that a lawyer had launched a lawsuit against me for a considerable sum. Besides the troubling development of one lawsuit, Kenny Sorosky made threats to sue me for disclosing the unethical and illegal scams he employed to bilk investors out of higher commissions. The irony was that, in an effort to pressure me, he even threatened to sue my 66-year-old unemployed mother because he surmised that she had typed my blogs and manuscripts. The imminent end to my imprisonment, I had to acknowledge, would not bring an end to my struggle. More to come.

Challenges in life would never cease. By anticipating them, however, we could empower ourselves to respond appropriately. I regret not having made better preparations for life following graduation from USC. I had more privileges than most, more opportunities to distinguish myself in positive ways, and to make meaningful contributions to the world. Instead of living up to my potential, my reflection while I served my time in prison convinced me that I had floundered.

I could not turn back the calendar pages, though like any person I could make better decisions as I moved forward. By recognizing the bad decisions of my past, I could take corrective actions. That understanding was the underlying reason that I studied so many writings in ethics and philosophy during the months I served in prison.

Between the time I graduated from college, and the time I surrendered to prison, I could not recall having read a single book. Against the sage advice I had received from my distinguished cousin, I pursued financial success. That myopic approach to life was what began my slide away from the values I had learned at home and as an athlete.

The readings and reflections that carried me through my sentence made a compelling case for a more balanced life. Besides the simple focus on work, career, and finances, I had to set goals that would not neglect my health and fitness, as well as my responsibilities to make contributions to the larger community. I could never allow apathy to creep in and contaminate my life again. With a constant pursuit of learning, I could prepare to respond well to whatever challenges might come next.

While I served my sentence, life moved on. Besides the difficulties like the passing of my dog, and being served with lawsuits that complicated my financial standing, our family grew with a new baby. I felt saddened that I could not celebrate the joy at home of learning that my brother Todd and my sister-in-law Sunny were going to have their first child.

An inability to participate fully in family affairs was one of the consequences of confinement. What I could do, however, was strive to prove myself worthy of the love I had received. Instead of self-pity for problems my own bad decisions had created, I could add meaning to my life by learning more, contributing to the lives of others, and preparing myself to make values-based decisions. Such a commitment would prepare me to live as a better son, a better brother, a better uncle. It would also help me live as a better husband once I found the woman with whom I would share my life.

Existentialist philosophers like Nietzsche, Sartre, and Heidegger wrote that man could overcome any obstacle. If he just had the courage to prepare, to face obstacles head on, to set meaningful goals, he could pick himself up from any predicament. Man could make himself stronger, better, more capable of meeting his challenges that were sure to come if he lived with more self-direction.

The 12-plus months I served in prison may not have been significant in relation to the totality of my life. They were profound, however, in the insight they brought. Whereas I had graduated college with the singular pursuit of a higher income, I didn't give a single thought to what I was becoming as a human being. As a consequence of my not having direction, or a strong center, without even knowing it, I let myself slide. I became heavy. I struggled with both low spirits and lethargy. I was envious, selfish, and shallow.

That lack of direction, together with misplaced goals and values, sent me on a course that could not help but lead to unhappiness. I lived a lie. Although I did not set out to scheme or defraud, neither did I exercise the good judgment or show the qualities of good character to prevent the fraud from perpetuating. Instead, I facilitated it. When caught, I compounded my problems by scheming to cover up my crimes.

My penance did not come from the year I served in prison. Penance came through the battles that played out in my mind and the lessons that ensued through introspection. I left prison ready, prepared for whatever adversity or challenges would come.

I was living a story, one from which others could learn. Rather than hide from shame, I would shine a light on the consequences that followed a disregard of ethics. Professors could offer students theoretical perspectives, and human resources departments could craft written corporate codes for employees to follow. As a man who had endured all aspects of the criminal justice system, I intended to offer perspectives from what others had taught me and from what I had experienced. In so doing, I knew that I could add value to society, helping others make better decisions before their lives tacked off course.

For those who did find themselves in the crosshairs of the criminal justice system, however, the information that follows would help them make better decisions.

21
Guide Through System

As a university student, and as a young executive in the financial sector, I would have welcomed more training in ethics. Particularly, I would have found value in listening to stories about the consequences that followed allegations of wrongdoing. Such information would have shaken me out of my complacency, and it may have checked my sense of entitlement.

I'd like to think that by reaching out I could make a connection with those audiences that I addressed. Perhaps when faced with ethical dilemmas of their own, those who listened to my presentation would have a clearer understanding of what could happen to those who began to compromise in their commitments to making values-based decisions.

Prior to my imprisonment I had a conversation with a journalist from a leading business magazine. During the interview, I expressed my opinion that the criminal justice system could ensnare anyone. The journalist took umbrage at my remark.

"I've been a journalist covering business for 20 years," he told me. "During that time I've never been tempted to break the law. That's why I'm intrigued with people who seem to disregard the rules by which others live."

My intentions were never to patronize those with whom I spoke. Certainly I recognized that my own character flaws were not an indictment of all in society. What I hoped to convey was that there was a time in my life that I, too, would have been offended at the suggestion that I was prone to criminal wrongdoing. I served time with hundreds of educated offenders who, like me, never envisioned the prospect of a criminal conviction. By describing what I learned, I simply hoped to contribute to the education of others.

As media reports showed every day, however, the criminal justice system was in no danger of extinction. Man has fallen to the allure of temptation since the beginning of recorded history. People of all walks of life would feel pressures of some sort. Those who perceived opportunities and lacked a full appreciation for the ramifications of their actions would continue to succumb to temptation of wrongdoing. They might even rationalize their actions and insist that they did not do anything wrong.

All that I have learned and observed from others, as well as what I have experienced, could prove of value to those people as well. Had I found access to such information while I was still employed at UBS, I would have made better decisions. By clinging to my steadfast denials and immersing myself in the lie, I truly aggravated my problems. What I learned as a defendant was that the best way to avoid problems with the criminal justice system was to live in accordance with the principles of good behavior. Those who crossed the line, however, would put themselves in the best possible position by accepting responsibility at the soonest possible time.

Take a lesson from the international scandal that surrounded Bernard Madoff. He had been a pillar of the financial community and one of Wall Street's most distinguished names. He also admitted to being one of the world's most effective con artists. Despite a massive and deliberate criminal scheme that made victims of thousands, prosecutors did not lock Madoff in a cell as a common criminal. Instead they allowed him to live in opulence while lawyers negotiated the most favorable sanction possible for a man who masterminded a $50 billion fraud.

There was a reason that the government allowed Madoff the privilege of quasi-freedom. It was because he had come forward and agreed to cooperate before law enforcement even suspected wrongdoing.

The sooner an individual accepted responsibility for his actions, the more likely he was to receive favorable consideration from the criminal justice system. Every day that passed after a crime took place exposed the defendant to deeper sanctions. I learned this lesson not only from reading the headlines of the Bernie Madoff scandal, but from personal experiences and from listening to the experiences of others.

Taylor was a pension-fund manager who served time with me at Taft Camp. He was responsible for the oversight of more than $100 million in retirement accounts. In an effort to make up for poor performance, Taylor began to camouflage results. His efforts deliberately mislead investors, and his deceptions were responsible for $20 million in losses.

After more than nine months of perpetuating the fraud, Taylor could not manage the stress. Authorities had no idea of his wrongdoing, and they were more than willing to accept Taylor's full cooperation. Taylor did not approach the authorities with a lawyer or with any requests for special deals. He simply laid all of his actions on their desk, explained his motivation and accepted what consequences followed.

Had Taylor not come forward, there was no telling how much time would have passed before authorities would have discovered the fraud. As a result of Taylor's full cooperation, acceptance of total responsibility, and total remorse, the system was much more lenient on him than it otherwise would have been. Taylor told me that he decided to come forward because the guilt was eating him up inside, and he couldn't take the pressure any longer.

I have not had any legal training, and I would never presume to disperse legal advice. Lawyers had a crucial role in our system of justice that could never be displaced. Rather than making a judgment call on Taylor's decision to come forward to authorities without legal counsel, my intention in telling his story was for readers to understand that the justice system treats those who cooperate freely with more leniency.

In my own case, readers should note the disparity in treatment between my former senior partner, Kenny Sorosky, and me. Whereas I told lies and took active steps to cover up my wrongdoing, Kenny took action. From that first moment that our supervisors at UBS called us in for questioning, Kenny understood that full cooperation would put him in the best light.

Kenny retained a top-notch criminal defense attorney. He told his lawyers everything he could about our relationship with Keith Gilabert's GLT Hedge Fund, including our complicity and the ways we profited from the fraud. Regardless of his motivations for coming forward, Kenny's lawyers succeeded in absolving him from a criminal prosecution and the huge financial sanctions that would have followed if he had not come forward. Most white-collar offenders delayed their acceptance of responsibility. Instead, they denied wrongdoing and tried to explain away their actions. Every day that passed, however, exposed defendants to more severe judgment from the system.

As prosecutors devoted more resources to a criminal case, the more vested they became. That was the reason they offered the most favorable consideration to those who came forward soonest. The worst decision a criminal defendant could make was to lie. I learned that the hard way.

When I initially retained counsel, I told him a story that completely cloaked my criminal wrongdoing. That ridiculous strategy may have been rooted in my humiliation, but it brought severe consequences.

I could not bring myself to come clean. It was as if by lying I could somehow retain a self-image of respectability that I so desperately wanted to maintain. Once I told one lie, I had to cover it up with another. In time, I wasn't only lying to my attorney, but also to government lawyers who insisted upon debriefing me. Without even comprehending the severity of my problems, I committed additional felonies with the lies I told.

Those who anticipated that they could become defendants in a criminal case could serve themselves best by understanding both the options available, and the ramifications that would follow the choices they made.

By not allowing myself to come to terms with the problems my decisions had created, I kept digging myself in deeper. Rather than acting assertively and working with a plan to bring about the best possible outcome, I was playing golf with my fingers crossed, ridiculously hoping that the government would be too busy to fiddle with what I perceived as a trifling matter.

From my own experience, and from what I learned by listening to others, I became convinced that too many defendants came into this system without a full appreciation for the cynicism and severity associated with every step in the process. Defendants wanted to believe that law enforcement officers, prosecutors, even the courts would understand. In the white-collar criminal defendant's mind, everyone in the system would recognize that he wasn't really a bad guy, and that he didn't deserve to be treated like a criminal. Such misperceptions make the defendant vulnerable to further problems.

The sooner a defendant accepted full responsibility, expressed remorse and demonstrated his contrition, the more he could influence his outcome. Those who believed investigators or prosecutors would identify with a criminal defendant, or that law enforcement officers would feel some sort of common humanity with him from the outset did not understand how justice was dispensed.

Those who made their profession in law enforcement identified with the losses of victims, not the struggles of criminal defendants. Justice to them meant a commitment to protect society and the people who suffered as a consequence of crime. Such a view conditioned those who worked in the law to attribute all actions by defendants to selfish motivations or self-preservation. Those who committed their careers to law enforcement listened as criminals told lies every day. Investigators asked questions that provoked defendants to incriminate themselves; the motive of law enforcement was to solve the case, not to ease the conscience of criminal defendants.

Too many defendants spoke with law enforcement officers in the same way I did. In the beginning, I felt certain that the government lawyers would see me for a nice guy. I lied with hopes that I could escape formal accusations of wrongdoing. The government knew that I was lying, but the investigators allowed me to continue. Each lie I told exposed me to further sanctions.

The many men with whom I spoke in prison convinced me that law enforcement officers relied upon a defendant's feeling of vulnerability. They were trained to ask questions in ways that would strengthen the prosecution's case, not to provide defendants with a way

179

Justin M. Paperny

out. The Fifth Amendment to the constitution provided American defendants with the right to withhold answers to questions by law enforcement. It did not excuse them from the sanctions that would come to those who lied.

Those of us who served time in federal prison learned such lessons too late. An individual did not have to answer questions by law enforcement officers. If he did, however, the individual would serve his interests best by either speaking with complete honesty or not saying anything at all.

Once an individual had reason to believe that he might become a target of a criminal investigation, he should seek guidance from legal counsel. That decision seemed obvious. Many men in prison, however, did not grasp the importance of working honestly with counsel. Like I did, they sought someone who would affirm delusions that they would be okay. What a criminal defendant needed was an attorney who would throw a bucket of ice-cold water on him and shake him into reality.

At the same time, defendants would serve themselves well by listening to others who had been through the gauntlet of justice. That meant personal experience with every aspect of the system. I learned more from my conversations with Walt Pavlo than I did from anyone else, and I wish that I had sought his counsel much earlier in the process. Talking with someone who had gone through the system did more than prepare defendants for what was ahead. Such conversations could also help an individual understand how decisions early in the process could influence outcomes that would not reveal themselves until years later.

Once an individual became a defendant, a time would come when he would have to either plead guilty or contest his innocence. The defendant should have complete trust with his attorney when he made such a pivotal decision. When I tried to lie my way through that polygraph test, my attorney sat me down and laid out the facts for me. "You're going to prison," he told me in no uncertain terms. "The best thing I can do for you now is to work out the most favorable deal possible."

If I had had enough foresight to speak honestly with my attorney from the outset, the resolution to my case would have been handled much sooner. As a consequence of the bad choices I made, I wasted hundreds of thousands of dollars; I made matters worse for those who loved me and supported me; I delayed the healing that could have begun much sooner.

Following a conviction, the defendant would have to participate in a presentence investigation. A probation officer would conduct the investigation, and it would culminate with a formal report known as the PSI. The PSI document would provide the judge with background information on the defendant, but it would have much more far-reaching consequences, as both the prison administrators and the probation department would rely upon the PSI for all future evaluations of the defendant.

I spoke with too many defendants in prison who told me that their attorneys did not grasp the ancillary significance of the PSI. Although the document might influence the sentence the judge imposed, the real importance of the PSI was the influence it would have with regard to the individual's confinement. Since most attorneys did not have intimate experience with the prison system, they could not anticipate the ways it would influence a defendant's confinement. In most cases, prison administrators would rely upon information in the PSI to determine where an individual would serve his time; in which programs they would allow him to participate; the type of work assignment and bunk assignment he would receive; and even the length of time they would authorize the defendant for halfway house time.

Those who had experience in progressing through confinement as prisoners were in the best position to shed light on such matters as the PSI's relevance. I met many people in prison who learned this reality the hard way. As a consequence of their proceeding blindly through the presentence investigation, they responded to questions in ways that exposed them to more difficult living conditions, and longer terms inside prison boundaries. Not knowing anything about prison, their attorneys only concerned themselves with the sentence that was going to be imposed.

The investigation began with a formal meeting between the defendant and the probation officer. The defense attorney was sometimes present for the meeting, but in other cases the defendant met with the probation officer alone. Either way, the defendant had to recognize the legal significance of the meeting. The probation officer would ask questions about the individual's background, and the probation officer would record the answers provided by the defendant.

Then the probation officer would investigate. Through that investigation the probation officer would make a determination as to whether the defendant was cooperative, accepting of responsibility, and remorseful. Those findings would have a definite influence on the sentence and the manner in which an individual served his sanction. As in all interactions with law enforcement officers, the defendant would be well served to understand the far-reaching consequences of the answers he provided.

After the PSI was completed, the next phase in the journey would be the sentencing hearing itself. Although defendants did not have the power to reverse prior decisions that led to a criminal conviction and sentencing, there were actions he could take in advance of sentencing that might mitigate the sanction imposed. Likewise, the defendant could behave in ways that would exacerbate the sentence. As a prisoner, I heard stories of both.

Gregg had been a successful CEO of a publicly traded corporation. In that capacity he had a duty to provide investors with accurate and timely information that detailed the financial health of his company. The government charged Gregg with fraud in an alleged scheme to pump up the excitement in his company, so that the share prices would rise, allowing him to profit while he unloaded millions of shares from his own account.

After his conviction, Gregg went public with his anger at the Justice Department. He claimed that the prosecutors were not interested in justice, but in securing convictions that would bring them national headlines. In interview after interview, Gregg asserted that he was a victim of investor hysteria. Markets had gone down, people had lost money, and prosecutors were scoring political points by bringing criminal charges against the rich. He said they were destroying capitalism, and that his conviction should be an outrage to every true American. Gregg assured the hosts of financial talk shows and reporters from the financial press that his company had been sound when he made his reports. The shares liquidated from his account were the result of margin calls, not some conniving scheme to enrich himself. He was a victim of market forces, just like everyone else.

Neither the probation officer, who was completing Gregg's presentence investigation, nor the U.S. Attorney was pleased with Gregg's public outburst. The government had made the case that Gregg authorized the liquidation of personal holdings he had in his company while he was publicly urging investors and employees to buy. That conflict resulted in his conviction for fraud, and he faced a prison term with a guideline range that capped out at five years.

As a response to Gregg's effort to lambaste the government in the media, Gregg's probation officer concluded that Gregg felt no remorse. She thought of him as an unrepentant manipulator of the public trust. The probation officer wrote him a scathing PSI. She wrote that Gregg had abused his position of authority to enrich himself, and that his outbursts in the media contributed to a lack of trust in financial markets. She urged the judge to enhance Gregg's sentence in response to his recalcitrance.

During the sentencing hearing, Gregg's prosecutor also urged the judge to depart upward from the sentencing guidelines because of Gregg's defiance. He had harmed the pursuit of justice with the media spectacle he created, the prosecutor insisted. Such actions were worthy of a more severe sanction than he otherwise would have received. The judge agreed and sentenced Gregg to serve seven years.

The merits of Gregg's argument were not as relevant as the forum he chose. Had he reserved his argument for the appeals court, the judge would have imposed a term that was within the guideline range. Gregg's public outrage thus cost him an additional two years in prison. In retrospect, he told me, the more prudent course would have been silence. The passion at the time inflamed Gregg, however, and he said he could not contain his rage. He signed up for anger-management courses in prison, but those classes were not going to erase the extra two years he served.

Geoff responded to his conviction differently from Gregg. Geoff was in the business of designing Web sites.

His small company advertised its services on Internet search engines and through direct marketing. Upon identifying customers, Geoff and his team worked with the client to design, build, and maintain effective Internet strategies to enhance the client's business.

One of Geoff's clients ordered a Web site that would attract prospective investors. Geoff worked with the client in designing the Web site, and then built the site in accordance with the client's expectations. Geoff did not know that the client had been using the Web site to fish for investors who would prove gullible enough to dump money into a Ponzi scheme.

Government prosecutors charged that Geoff should have known that his client was promising unrealistic returns to investors under the doctrine of "willful blindness"; the prosecutors charged Geoff with being complicitous in the fraud. Geoff insisted that he did not know anything about his client's scheme to defraud investors. As far as Geoff knew, he said that he was building a Web site for a legitimate business. Nevertheless, to spare himself the possibility of a lengthy prison term, Geoff accepted a plea agreement that exposed him to a prison term of between two and three years.

Unlike Gregg, Geoff did not rail against the government with accusations of injustice. Geoff did the opposite. He volunteered to speak at local business organizations to describe what he had learned about corporate responsibility. Geoff used his story as a tool to help other businessmen understand their duty to know more about their clients. Those speaking engagements led Geoff to work with inner-city kids who had been marked as at-risk adolescents. He not only spoke with them about his imminent prison term, he mentored several on the consequences that followed bad decisions. Geoff then used contacts he had in the computer industry to donate computers and software so that he could set up a workshop facility that would train the at-risk adolescents in developing computer skills. Geoff's selfless efforts to make contributions to society impressed his probation officer. During her presentence investigation, the probation officer learned that Geoff had been volunteering his time and energy to help improve society. She believed that Geoff's efforts demonstrated a commitment to reconcile with the community. As a result of that assessment, the probation officer suggested that a downward adjustment from the sentencing guidelines might be appropriate in Geoff's case to reward his post-conviction rehabilitation.

At sentencing, the judge agreed with the probation officer's assessment. The prosecutor did not object. Instead of imposing a term of between two and three years, as called for by sentencing guidelines, Geoff's judge imposed a split sentence of ten months. Geoff was to serve five months at Taft Camp, where I met him, and five months of home confinement.

Following the PSI report would come the sentencing hearing itself. Our adversarial system of justice would require the prosecution to present its best case for the appropriate sanction. Then the defense attorney would counter with a case on reasons why the defendant should receive some type of consideration for mitigating circumstances. The episode was like a well-choreographed and predictable script, with prosecutors asking for more severe sentences, and defense attorneys arguing for leniency.

Judges presided over such sentencing hearings as a regular function of their responsibility. They were expected to listen to both sides without bias, and then rely upon their wisdom and discretion to impose a sentence that was in accordance with law. Defendants would be well served to understand the gravity associated with the sentencing hearing.

I was well advised prior to my sentencing hearing. My attorney told me that I could put myself in a more favorable light through voluntary efforts to make amends. I did the best I could, and the judge noticed.

Other prisoners I met regretted that they did not play a more active role in preparation for their sentencing hearings. Instead of participating at all, they stood mute before the court, allowing their defense attorneys to express the reasons that warranted leniency. My assessment from listening to others suggested that defendants could serve their interests better by taking proactive steps to demonstrate their remorse.

A good consultant could help with sentencing preparations. Consultants could work with defendants to prepare them for both the presentence investigation, and for the sentencing hearing. Judges were accustomed to listening to defense attorneys expound upon the virtues of their clients. What they heard far less frequently were expressions of sincere remorse from defendants themselves. Sentencing consultants could help the defendant compile sentencing packages and coach them to deliver effective presentations during the hearing itself.

Following the sentencing hearing the defendant must be prepared to encounter the prison system. Proper preparations would ensure that he not only survived prison, but that he thrived through prison.

My having spoken with Walt before self-surrendering truly helped. I could identify with Walt's background. Like I was, Walt was a college-educated executive who had never expected to serve a day in prison. Bad decisions led to criminal convictions and prison terms

Justin M. Paperny

for both of us. Since he had gone through it all before, I found real value in speaking with him prior to beginning my term.

I had asked my attorney what prison was going to be like. He couldn't answer in a way that would prepare me for the journey. I had read a book on the experiences of climbing Mount Everest. Yet if an aspiring mountain climber wanted to undertake the journey of climbing the world's tallest mountain, he would do better to speak with someone who had reached the peak rather than seek information from someone like me who had only read about someone else's experiences.

The worst parts about prison, I came to learn, were the months of anxiety that preceded it. Those who didn't understand anything about life inside had a rougher go of the initial journey. They began their terms with the misperception that life in prison would be the same as life outside. It was not. There were rules, both written and unwritten. Not knowing and understanding them could lead to altercations with both prisoners and staff members. Those altercations could result in longer and more onerous terms than necessary.

Some of the lessons I learned from the other prisoners who began their terms without having a clue about prison culture were that some lived with too many misperceptions that were delivered through popular media, and that inappropriate adjustments at the outset could lead to an avalanche of problems.

The basic incoming process was an uncomfortable routine of paperwork, fingerprints, photographs, interviews and inspections. It was somewhat demeaning, but foreknowledge of it all helped steel me for the few hours of discomfort. As far as life in prison was concerned, those admission rituals hardly mattered at all. What did make a

Lessons From Prison

difference, on the other hand, was the way an individual adjusted as soon as he stepped onto the prison compound.

Even in a minimum-security camp, everyone's eyes would be on the new guy. Some of the prisoners would have come from professional backgrounds, but others would be prisoners who had served many years or even decades of their lives inside prison boundaries. It was best for incoming prisoners to understand that a basic social structure existed, and those who violated prison protocols did so at their own peril.

I was fortunate in my adjustment. I had a better understanding of what to expect because of my conversations with Walt before self-surrendering. Besides those informed consultations, I met some nice people within my first minutes at Taft Camp. People like David, Arthur, and Michael helped my adjustment.

After I had been at Taft Camp for several months, I had the privilege of leading a class designed by Scott Evans, an inspirational leader from Los Angeles who volunteered his time by teaching courses in the prison. Scott had designed a course that he called the Entrepreneurial Compass. Through that course, participants learned how to transcend adversity by setting clearly identifiable goals. In facilitating the course during the weeks Scott was away, I was able to help other prisoners figure out strategies to make the most productive use of their time. Those who lacked such guidance sometimes crossed lines from which there seemed no return.

Tom told me about his difficult journey. We had struck up a conversation while we were in the library. Tom said that he had worked as a computer programmer and that his conviction for software piracy led to a three-year term. He self-surrendered to the camp at Lompoc, but within his first week he had become labeled the camp snitch.

189

Justin M. Paperny

Tom's problem began in the community television room, he said. He was watching a news program, when another prisoner walked up and changed the channel to a reality show. Tom said that he took a stand, asserting that he had been watching the news. The other prisoners responded by taunting Tom. Feeling threatened, he said that he walked away from the television room directly to the officer's desk and reported the altercation.

"I had only been in the camp for a few days," Tom said. "I didn't want any problems. Speaking with the guard seemed like a better approach than accepting the other prisoner's challenge to a fight."

The officer locked Tom in segregation. Tom did not want to go, and he did not understand why the guards were punishing him for doing what seemed like the right thing. The prisoner who challenged Tom was also sent to segregation, and administrators transferred the aggressor to the higher-security prison. After a few weeks, Tom said he returned from segregation to Lompoc Camp. By then, his reputation as a snitch had been indelibly etched in stone.

There were 350 inmates confined in Lompoc, Tom told me, and he said that he felt as if every one of the other prisoners were conspiring against him. He exaggerated, of course, but the year Tom served there seemed unbearable. He would return from his work assignment and find that while he was gone, other inmates had poured urine on his pillow or smeared feces inside his sheets. He said that he did not feel safe, as he had enemies that he couldn't even identify.

On two separate occasions, Tom turned himself in to the guards for protective custody. That status meant that he was locked inside a cell, without access to a telephone or to recreational activities. He had hoped that the animosity would die. It did not. Each time the administrators returned Tom to the camp, the harassments began anew.

Tom served his first year under the difficult conditions. Then he was successful in transferring to Taft Camp, where he hoped to begin serving his sentence as one of the low-key inmates who seemed to move through the prison with anonymity. He was not so fortunate. Apparently, there were other prisoners at Taft Camp who had been at Lompoc Camp while Tom was a lightening rod. They quickly spread the word that Tom was a snitch.

Writing about prison adjustment patterns would require volumes of literature, much more space than a small book could provide. I served nearly 400 days in a federal prison. Through my blog at JustinPaperny.com, I tried to record much of my daily life. Each day of my journey, however, provided me with enough experiences to lead seminars on the importance of preparation.

To master the time inside prison boundaries, an individual needed to envision how he wanted to emerge. If he could start serving his time with that clear picture of how he wanted to walk out of prison then he could select the adjustment plan that would work best for him. Those who began serving their time without a plan, unfortunately, sometimes made bad decisions like Tom. In those cases, circumstances would complicate the adjustment, and prison would become a living hell.

If a person knew how he wanted to emerge from prison, then he could set clear goals in place. Those goals should have meaning and contribute to the individual's overall life purpose. Those who focused only on getting through the sentence often found that they reached the end with an entire new set of anxieties that would hinder their ability to re-enter society. Thriving through prison required preparation.

Preparation began by developing a clear understanding of the prison environment. Tom wanted others to understand him before he had any idea of how the subcultures that dominate inside prison environments operated. Believing that he had to take a stand with the television led to his severe adjustment problem. His choice may have seemed an obvious lack of discretion, but during the time I served in prison I saw scores of prisoners who served difficult terms because of poor choices they made once inside prison boundaries.

By understanding the environment, and understanding the way he wanted to emerge, the individual could chart a course that would lead to success. I had help. That help led me to turning my year in prison into one of the most productive periods of my life. I became physically fit, emotionally sound, spiritually balanced, and intellectually prepared. As a consequence of my adjustment, I thrived through prison, and walked out of those gates much stronger than when I walked in. Preparation was the reason behind my successful journey.

Epilogue

During those mid-days of spring 2008, I walked into the federal prison in Taft with a very different mindset. I was overweight, and I felt threatened by the challenges of the 18-month sentence I was scheduled to serve. As I came closer to the spring of 2009, however, I felt as if the Justin Paperny who was walking out of prison was far different from the Justin Paperny who had walked in.

Although I began with delusions that I wouldn't make it through, my time in prison had come to an end. In the final weeks, I read about the severe economic crisis that was plaguing our country and spreading. Government statistics showed that with more than 11 million people out of work, the unemployment rate exceeded 8 percent. Another 20 million people were underemployed, working jobs that were beneath their qualifications. The times were far more challenging than when I began serving my time.

When I self-surrendered, I knew what Walt had told me about prison, but nothing more. As I completed my term, I knew that I would be walking into another scene of unfamiliarity. I was returning to what I had read was the most challenging economy since the Great Depression, and I would have the stigma of being an ex-convict with a felony blemishing my resume. If the unemployment rate in America was 8 percent, I expected that it exceeded 50 percent for people who had just walked out of prison.

Besides the financial torrents through which I would have to swim, I was releasing from prison to a halfway house. Once there, I'd be assigned to yet another strange bed that had been occupied by hundreds or thousands of derelicts before me. I'd have to adjust to new conditions of confinement, both interacting with and sharing

Justin M. Paperny

bathroom and eating space with a new group of strangers, all of whom had felonies and challenges of their own.

My term in prison had come to an end, though three years of what was known as supervised release awaited me. I'd met several men in Taft Camp who were serving time because their probation officers had cited them with violating the terms of their conditional release. They described horror stories of living in society with limitations that would require them to submit to continuous scrutiny and oversight.

Regardless of what I'd heard about supervised release, life in the halfway house, or what I read about the wicked job market awaiting me, I was walking out of prison with total confidence and optimism. The preparations I had made assured me that I could navigate my way through whatever challenges were to come. With the lessons I had learned, I felt certain that I would thrive through all adversity. Moving forward, I would always make values-based decisions, pursuing happiness by keeping everything I did, everything I said, and everything I thought in harmony.

My strength was rooted in a clear understanding of the values by which I would live. I knew that challenges awaited me. They would always await me. More to come. Yet I also knew what I had just completed. During a single year in prison I had brought both balance and discipline to my life. Through exercise, I worked myself into excellent physical shape. By contemplating how I wanted to emerge from prison, I set a schedule and work ethic that allowed me to connect with thousands through the written word. I came to live by the motto, "if you say you're going to do something, you do it." Introspection and readings in philosophy opened my mind, imbuing a deeper sense of purpose with which I could move forward.

Lessons From Prison

Greed and misdirection were the character flaws that had brought me to prison. My misdeeds, my crimes as a money manager, were symptoms or indications that I was on a course of self-destruction, making victims of others. That was the past; it was what got me here.

I was leaving prison with a better understanding of the world, a better grasp of my relationship to others, and more appreciation for the responsibilities that came with good citizenship. Those realizations assured me that I would live with more balance. The new foundation that had come with my deliberate adjustment through confinement gave me a perspective that I did not have before. I felt stronger because of it. I knew that I could rely on my new perspective to get there.

Yes, I would encounter struggles. So what? Struggles, I had come to accept, were part of life. The answers were not to be found through double cheeseburgers and online chess. I could never allow adversity to cripple me, no matter how bad the pain. I had to persevere, as I had learned in coping through the loss felt with the death of my dog.

Through my adjustment to prison, I learned that I could handle struggle just fine. I would learn what conditions or expectations both the halfway house and probation officer would have for me, and I would live in compliance. I would evaluate the tough economic conditions outside. Through my understanding, I felt confident that I could create opportunities that would add value to the lives of others. I knew that I would find my place in the world.

There was a lot I had left behind, and a lot had changed during the year I had been away. Decisions I had made were responsible for separating me from the lives of friends, family, and community. I looked forward to

195

proving myself worthy of the support I received from all as I returned to society, a better man because of my experiences.

Friendship came with responsibilities, and in making decisions that had led me into troubles with the criminal justice system, I had let my friends down. Felony convictions carried a stigma, yet despite the disgrace that came with my troubles, my friends stood by me in ways that both humbled and strengthened me.

Whereas my business partner had gone into self-preservation mode, hanging me in the process, my friend Sam Pompeo stepped up to bolster my spirits. Despite the termination of my employment at UBS, Sam insisted that I join his real estate practice as a full partner. He defended me to colleagues when the Department of Justice released press announcements that humiliated me as a felon before the Los Angeles business community.

Sam's friendship carried me through that tumultuous period between my firing at UBS and my self-surrender to prison. I needed strength then and Sam delivered. As a consequence of his standing proudly beside me during a time of need, I was able to grow through my confinement. The growth I made brought me a new sense of appreciation for the meaning of friendship. It meant more than accepting the support that others generously gave. Friendships came with the responsibility of reciprocating, and I looked forward to rebuilding my friendship with Sam as I walked out of prison boundaries.

Likewise with Brad Fullmer. Brad had been like a brother to me since childhood. While I served my prison term, he stood right there beside me. Despite the round trip drive of several hours, Brad and his wife Elana visited me regularly while I served my sentence. They wanted to ensure my spirits were strong. I appreciated the numerous ways they reached out to me through my journey. As I walked out of prison, I felt stronger because of their friendships, and I looked forward to joining them at home.

Besides my friends, I had an incredibly loving family to which I was returning. Each member inspired me to work towards becoming a better man as I served my sentence, and I felt a debt of gratitude for their support.

My mother Tallie and Ken, my stepfather, and my father Bernie, and my stepmother Ronda, served this sentence along with me. My parents never imagined that they would be visiting a son in prison, yet they endured the humiliation of sitting in a room full of felons, holding and embracing me as if I were deserving of their pride. I loved my parents deeply, and I felt a sense of duty to live the rest of my years as a son who would prove worthy of such support.

My family members did not deserve the shame. As I served my sentence, I realized how many victims both my crime and my initial response to it had caused. At first I was blind to the widespread fallout. All I thought about was how my own life was falling apart. While in prison, I saw the bigger picture.

By engaging in behavior that violated the universal code of right and wrong, I contributed to a fraud that cost millions. My actions influenced a diminishing trust in the public markets. Family and friends had to endure the shame of reading about my crimes in newspapers. My dear mother had to read about it over and over while typing my daily blog entries that I sent home. And each family member suffered the humiliation willingly as they drove to the prison, submitting themselves to rules and inspections in order to sit across a table from me.

On 22 January 2009, my 34th birthday, my brother Todd and his wife Sunny brought a special gift to our family. That was the day that Sunny gave birth to Clover, my niece. I was running the track on the morning of Clover's birth, with tears of both joy and sadness falling. I was elated to have a niece, but saddened that crimes I had committed resulted in my not being able to celebrate together with family on the momentous occasion of my brother and sister-in-law's first child.

As I concluded my time in prison, I walked out realizing that I was returning to a loving family. That privilege was an honor that came with obligations. I could never allow myself to fall off course again. Instead of concerning myself with the selfish motivations that led to so much shame, I owed a duty to live in accordance with the principles of good citizenship.

Through this recalibration, I intended not only to prove myself worthy of the love I had received from family, but also to find the woman to whom I would devote my life. I was 34-years-old when I concluded my prison term. The self-absorbed life I lived prior to confinement did not suit me well for a committed relationship. I was walking out of prison with a new set of values, one that brought a new sense of meaning to my life.

Whereas I had once shunned what I had presumed to be the fetters of commitment, and sabotaged relationships whenever I sensed a woman who was coming too close, I was leaving prison a new man. Instead of focusing on my own wants and desires, I looked forward to finding and nurturing a love that would last forever. I had lived alone for far too long, and while suffering through the loss of Honey, I realized the incompleteness of my life.

Besides the year I served alone in prison, those readings of philosophy together with introspection helped me realize how empty life was without a woman to share it. I didn't know where or when I would find her, though in the loneliness of my prison rack, I thought about the woman who would become my wife. I wanted to see her, to know her, to touch, and to feel her. At the same time, I was glad that she was enjoying a real life somewhere, and not suffering through my imprisonment along with my family members I had hurt.

As I walked out of prison, I knew that my life was about to begin. Everything I had done up until that point was in preparation for what was to come. I had made some bad decisions, but the lessons that had come from them, I knew, promised to make me a better man. I was ready to live as a good friend, a good son, a good brother, a good uncle and in time, an excellent husband and father.

I also recognized my responsibility to live as a good citizen, and that meant making contributions to society. Walt had given of himself through his public speaking to universities and businesses. Instead of allowing the disgrace to die and build a new life, he offered his story to others, exposing himself to a life of ridicule so that others could learn the consequences that follow unethical behavior. Reading about such lessons could not compare to the interactive lessons Walt offered audiences by talking about what he had learned from his crime.

I admired Walt's courage in telling his story to audiences across the world, though I knew he paid a heavy price in not allowing the past to settle. I had an opportunity to sit for an interview that Professor Kelly Richmond Pope coordinated. She taught business courses and the importance of ethics to students in the graduate school at DePaul University. Kelly's colleague, Karen Chodzicki, joined a film crew who flew out from Chicago to the Taft Prison Camp to record my responses to questions. I opened up, describing the humiliating details of my crime with hopes that others could learn from my lessons. The exercise

199

was part of my atonement. As I walked out of prison, I didn't know whether I could continue telling the story of my shame, though Walt's commitment to contribute to the education of others inspired me.

I knew that I would have to find employment to sustain myself, though I sensed an obligation to offer my experiences to others. That was part of my redemption, and the motivation for waking each morning before three. I needed to memorialize all that I had learned through my nearly 400 nights as a prisoner. The energy invested was therapeutic, and I hoped that others would find value in the work.

In returning to my community, away from prison as a quasi-free man, I knew that I had values to live as a good man. As I had learned from the writings of that great American educator John Dewey, the good man was he who, regardless of what bad he had done in the past, was committed to living in ways that would make society better. I was ready. My contributions to society would come through the lessons I could offer, and the example I would live moving forward.